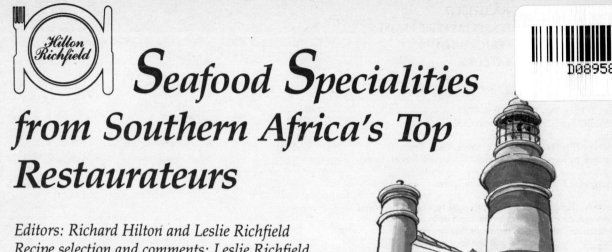

Seafood Specialities from Southern Africa's Top Restaurateurs

Editors: *Richard Hilton and Leslie Richfield*
Recipe selection and comments: *Leslie Richfield*
Design and illustrations: *Richard Ward*
Recipe Consultant: *Paula Blacking*
(Food Editor: "Living in South
Africa" magazine)

© 1986 Hilton-Richfield Publications
PO Box 262, Rondebosch 7700
PO Box 52799, Saxonwold 2132

HILTON-RICHFIELD
SEAFOOD SPECIALITIES FROM
SOUTH AFRICA'S TOP
RESTAURATEURS

Richard Hilton, PO Box 262, Rondebosch 7700
Leslie Richfield, PO Box 52799, Saxonwold 2132

Typeset by Diatype (Pty) Ltd, Roodehek Street, Cape Town
Litho reproduction by Reprotique (Pty) Ltd, Roodehek Street, Cape Town
Printed by Intergrafis, 105 Hope Street, Cape Town

Book trade orders (all areas except Cape Town)
MOBILE MAPS AND BOOKS (cc)
PO Box 2332, Edenvale 1610
Telephone: (011) 452-1464
(Cape Peninsula orders: 77-4610)

Contents

Please note that the restaurants participating are entered strictly alphabetically, to ensure fairness. If, perchance, you are used to turning first to the back of a book to see how it ends, start with the Zoo Lake Restaurant and work your way forward! You'll lose nothing by it.

Richard Hilton

Leslie Richfield

RICHARD HILTON and LESLIE RICHFIELD had a tremendous success three years ago with their book WINING, DINING AND WHERE TO STAY, which was South Africa's first (and only) comprehensive, critical guide to all the restaurants and hotels of South Africa.

The guide was top of the paperback best-sellers list in every centre of the Republic, and continued to sell well even when a great many of the facts and figures in it were out of date. Not everyone in the catering trade was entirely pleased with it and the authors came in for considerable criticism themselves – and a few threats of lawsuits, too!

RICHARD HILTON is the publisher and editor of SA RES-TAURANT, a magazine for the hospitality industry that is widely read. He has a lifelong interest in food and drink and has been connected with gastronomic publishing in Europe.

He has travelled extensively throughout southern Africa, visiting hotels and restaurants large and small, carefully noting changing trends in eating and drinking habits in our cities and towns and even in the remotest dorps.

LESLIE RICHFIELD is one of the best-known professional gourmets in South Africa. He frequently appears on television

This is the "blazon" of the world's biggest and most important gastronomical society, La Confrérie de la Chaîne des Rôtisseurs, founded in France in the year 1248. With its headquarters in Paris, it has members in 106 countries, of which South Africa is one.

This sign displayed outside a restaurant indicates that two senior members of the staff are Professional Members of the Chaîne.

at gastronomic events, and broadcasts regularly on food topics.

He is the National Gastronomic Counsellor of the prestigious French international gourmet society, La Chaîne des Rôtisseurs, and was one of the founders of the society in South Africa.

He is a member of the SA Chefs Association and a frequent speaker at catering trade seminars. His biting criticisms of bad food have made him some enemies, but he has a loyal public following who enjoy his outspokenness.

*I*ntroduction

*H*ave you ever dined at a restaurant, admired some particular dish, and wondered whether you could do it yourself, at home? Most people have done so at some time or another, and restaurants generally are flattered and pleased if you ask them for a recipe.

Trouble is, restaurant chefs don't have their recipes written out, all ready to be handed to some eager diner; nor are their recipes ever written in the style to which home cooks are accustomed. In London, many years ago, the famous restaurant Oddeninos and, later, The White House in Regents Park, used to have recipes printed on paper shaped to the type of food: a beef recipe was given to you on a printed sheet shaped like an ox, fishy recipes on fish-shaped paper, and so on.

That's taking it a bit too far, no doubt, but it illustrates the general attitude of chefs all over the world, when asked to divulge their secrets to "amateurs". They are glad to — because there are very few secrets in the culinary field, and it's the cooking, not the recipe, that makes the dish.

A culinary routine in the hands of one cook, turns out quite differently for another. It is this that probably gives rise to the old wives' tale that women, when giving each other recipes, deliberately leave out a vital ingredient, or a certain step, or put the timing wrong, or whatever, so that her "friend" won't get it quite right.

We refuse to believe this dreadful slur on the honesty and decency of our women-folk. And if it should ever be proved true of some women, we don't want to know about it. We are men of a certain age, perhaps a little old-fashioned in our attitudes, particularly towards women, whom we still often refer to as "the ladies", and we would rather keep our dreams intact, thank you.

The principal reason why the recipes of our excellent South African chefs are not more generally known by home cooks is that, until now, no-one has bothered to collect them and present them in suitable form. This book is an attempt to do just that.

It is not intended, though, to be a Book of the Gospel for aspirant home cooks, with each detail meticulously set down, every instruction presented in monotonous detail, everything in a certain order in its proper place, in exact and precise quantities, down to the nearest 0,5 of a gram.

This book is not the work of a careful home economist. We have read a number of those, and we get the impression from some of them that the writers imagine most of their readers are morons. We don't believe that.

If the ingredients are set down without omitting any, it doesn't matter if they are not in the order of use: the average home cook can soon sort that out for herself . . . or, in a growing number of instances, himself. And a pinch more of this, or a pinch less of that, usually won't make a scrap of difference to the way the dish turns out.

We find it atrocious, though, to have to be bound by certain laws of the country that we think are pretty silly. We refer to the metric regulations. Metrication is fine, modern, useful and fully accepted. There are still millions of people in south Africa who are over 35 years of age, however, and who see nothing wrong in

5

a book referring to "a teaspoonful" or "a tablespoon" or "half a cupful".

It's against the law, though, to write these terms — unless you put the metric equivalents first in milligrams or millilitres. Even the abbreviations you use are laid down. You shouldn't write "ml", for example, for millilitres, but "mℓ". And you can't give oven temperatures in Fahrenheit any more, as so many older readers are used to. No, you have to write Centigrade, or Celsius, although we understand that we shan't be sent to jail — yet! — if we put the F figure after the C in the recipes. And we wonder what the metric equivalent is for "a pinch"?

Unfortunately, the gulf between the professional kitchen and the home kitchen is a very wide one. The professional chef seldom measures his quantities meticulously. He is cooking more dishes for far more people than the average home cook, and he puts in a handful of this, a pinch of that, correcting if he has to during the cooking process.

He has other important things on his mind that never worry the home cook: portion control, food costs, productivity, kitchen security, hygiene (an inspector can walk in at any moment), staff control, and that dreadful institution that employers and accountants live by, the "bottom line".

His timing is different from the home cook's, too. In his preparation, usually long before the service period, he has to cover all the items on his à la carte menu, and the full range of dishes if it is a set menu he has to plan for. Perhaps the most dramatic illustration of the difference is the way a home cook watches just a few pots, with just three or four dishes having to be ready in time. Watch the bustle and frenetic activity in a professional kitchen, though, when a dozen or two dozen à la carte portions, each of a different kind, are all cooking together!

So professional chefs are not used to laying out recipes for the housewife. In fact, during the preparation of this book, we found only two who knew how to write the ingredients and the method so that the average homebody could follow it.

Nearly every recipe submitted to us, therefore, had to be re-written to some extent, and here we want to pay tribute to Paula Blacking, who has performed prodigious feats under pressure in trying to give our confused copy some semblance of intelligence. Paula has not tested the recipes, however. Hardly necessary, we thought. It would be insulting and time-wasting to cook and test recipes supplied by some of the master-chefs of our land. Most of our work has been editorial only.

We have been presumptuous enough, though, to put in a little comment or tip of our own after each recipe. No doubt none of these has anything new to say to our readers, but here and there perhaps some assistance may result. These comments and suggestions are from our own cooking experience in our own homes, and we accept responsibility for them. If some of them cause howls of derision from our esteemed colleagues, the corps of home economists, well — what's life without a little laughter?

The restaurants featured in this book were invited to participate by Richard Hilton or Leslie Richfield personally. We know them all, we trust them all. We would have liked to have included several more — indeed, scores more. Space and price and time were considerations against that. We wanted to keep the price down to a level where people would buy the book, not just leave it to languish on a bookshop's shelves, alongside all those glossy and beautiful volumes costing the earth. We want to be read — and enjoyed.

Readers may be surprised to note the number of hotel restaurants we have included. This is because in the past three or four years a revolution has taken place in the kitchens of most hotel chains.

Previously, food was served mainly to stop guests from feeling hungry. Now, the food operation is seen as something vital to the hotel's reputation, and important enough for the group to spend money, imagination and the brains of some of our finest food executives on the job. Hotel restaurants today are encouraged to be individual, to excel as far as they can, within a limited cost range, of course.

Some of them are extraordinary: innovative, creative and always offering something interesting and — above all — excellent in quality. The wise men in charge of our hotel groups are using brilliant chefs, whom they have plucked out of the kitchen and turned into equally capable executives: men of the calibre, for instance, of Bill Gallagher of Southern Sun and Bill Stafford of Protea Hotels & Inns.

So, before you proceed to the rest of this book, please be reminded once again that this is not meant to be your conservative, academic-type cook-book. If you find that some of the recipes seem a little similar to others, please remember that this indicates the narrow range of types of fish available in South Africa, especially inland, and the even narrower spectrum of the average South African's tastes in restaurant fare.

We would particularly like to thank artist Richard Ward for his beautiful illustrations. We know they will be much admired. And, again, our felicitations to Paula Blacking, whose vast knowledge of the kitchen and of cookery and nutrition, whose sense of humour and whose generosity and quick intelligence have helped us tremendously.

Thanks also to Stanley Dorman of Mariner's Wharf, for his encouragement and advice.

RICHARD HILTON
LESLIE RICHFIELD

About fish

It's not easy to write an introduction to a book about fish and sea-food recipes without repeating what has been said again and again in the past. So let's get the fundamentals out of the way with a few bald statements, such as:

1. Fish is good for you. It has lots of protein, as much as meat has. It's easily digestible. It has no or low cholesterol (except for some shellfish which is loaded with the stuff). Contrary to what mothers have been telling their children all these years, fish doesn't build or strengthen the brain to any marked degree rather than other parts of the body.

2. Until recent years, it was difficult to buy fresh fish if you lived inland. (And if you could, it might have been unwise. That great South African character and comedian, the late Cecil Wightman of "Snoektown Calling" fame, once said to the writer, in an exaggerated accent, "Man, I never eats fish north of Paarl". But that was 30 years ago.)

3. Up-country fish-lovers should be grateful to the big companies like Sea Harvest and Irvin & Johnson, who have spent millions in enabling the land-locked to enjoy really fresh fish. They should also be grateful to the small, unsung entrepreneurs who drive from the Transvaal down to the coast every week, bringing back loads of freshly-caught linefish. One or two of them are actually doing this legally!

4. Despite all this, South Africans eat far less fish than their counterparts overseas. This is probably because the average South African only knows three fish dishes: fish and chips, fish and chips, and fish and chips.

(The preceding statement is a gross exaggeration. If it were true, no-one would buy this book.)

The truth is that fish is as versatile a product as any other, when it comes to methods of cookery and the limitless range of variations in sauces and garnishes.

However, ask the average housewife how many ways of cooking a sole she knows, and if she's honest she'll say perhaps half a dozen or so. The more expert home cook (and we have many thousands of them in our land) might know up to 20 or 30 sole recipes. If you look up "sole", though, in that wonderful little reference book Hering (The Hering Dictionary of Classical and Modern Cookery) you'll see no less than 492 recipes under that heading.

Shopping for fish is not always simple. If the average housewife's shopping is confined to the local supermarket's fish counter, and if she insists on buying only fresh fish, and not the frozen variety, chances are she'll have a regular choice of only hake or kingklip. Fresh soles are sometimes there, too, and seasonal fish such as snoek, yellowtail, kabeljou, stumpnose and the rest occasionally appear. She can immediately tell the fresh fish from the frozen sort – by the price! Unfortunately, if you want your fish really fresh, you have to pay for it.

Sometimes, even if the price is high enough to persuade you that the fish really must be fresh, you might have the feeling, one Monday morning, that this is the same cold-eyed creature that faced you on the counter on Friday last. If you ask "Is it fresh?", the well-meaning assistant is sure to say "Yes, madam", meaning that, to the best of his knowledge, it has never been frozen. It does not imply, however, that it has just come in. For all you know, it might have been kept in the store's refrigerator for a few days.

All the best books tell you how to distinguish fresh fish from older stock – the smell, the state of the eyes, the firmness of the flesh and so on. Really fresh fish has hardly any smell or no smell at all. Not every housewife, though, has the nerve or the inclination to pick the thing up and sniff at it, to poke it about with her finger to see if the flesh is resilient, to stare into the poor creature's eyes for evidence of its recent demise.

So there are two things you can do. One: find out the days on which deliveries of fresh fish are made to the store, and confine your shopping to those days. Two: ask to see the delivery note. We have found, too, that if you shop regularly in one place, the assistants come to know you and to realise that you're not one to be fobbed off with inferior goods. Buying fish from them becomes a transaction between two mutually watchful parties.

A good policy is to find a smaller store that specialises in supplying really fresh fish. In Johannesburg, the famous Sea-Breeze Fisheries in Plein Street is one, and the more recently established but highly successful Fisherman's Deli in Dunkeld West, and the aptly named The Old Trout in Hyde Park, are others. Most other cities also have their speciality fish shops.

Now, for the first time in South Africa, there's another category of fresh fish available. Woolworths supermarkets, whose reputation in South Africa for high quality foods is as impressive as that of Marks & Spencer in Britain (who of course have a close connection with our Woolies) are now selling portions of fish, guaranteed fresh and never frozen, in skin-tight plastic wrapping. These pre-packed items are principally kingklip and hake, but the range is being extended to include fresh fish portions al-

ready coated and seasoned ready for cooking, and some even ready-stuffed and sauced.

We shall be able to rely on their quality and freshness because Woolworths imposes the strictest quality control measures in the country. No store is allowed to keep stocks for more than a couple of days and, incredible as it may seem to land-locked South Africans, when you buy this Woolworths pre-packed fish it can never be more than a few days out of the sea!

Woolies also have a big range of packaged, prepared and frozen fish, some of which they import from Britain under the "St Michael" label, and it's all very, very good indeed. You pay a trifle more, but for that reliable Woolworths quality no-one ought to mind.

The two giants, Sea Harvest and Irvin & Johnson, virtually control the fish sold by the Big Four supermarket chains. Not only do they distribute it, they actually catch most of it in their own trawlers. It's understandable that most of their product is the deep-sea varieties of fish: the kingklip, the stockfish and the sole. Big business has to have a regular and reliable source of supply, and the shoals of kingklip and hake (under any of its aliases, such as stockfish, haddock, etc) are usually pretty dependable.

One can't say the same for linefish, though. With them, you're in the lap of the sea-gods to a large extent. Only when the catch is large enough do the giants of the wet fish trade send supplies inland.

So it is that smaller companies are involved in the catching and despatching of kabeljou, red roman, steenbras, elf and the others. The small boats face a hundred-and-one possibilities every time they put to sea. (One such possibility is the landing of a few 74, said by many to be the finest fish in the sea. When was the last time you saw one, whether you live inland or at the coast?)

One of the biggest of the minor shippers of fish is a farmer from Honeydew, north of Johannesburg. John Harrison has a 20-tonne truck, nitrogen-cooled, which is driven down to the coast every week, buying up small catches and returning late on Sunday evenings. Early on a Monday morning, to see the concrete floor of the Harrisons' barn covered with containers of the freshest fish that ever found its way to the Transvaal, is something of a cultural shock.

But not every week is Christmas, even for a professional operator. Sometimes the catch just isn't very good, due to the weather, or seasonal disturbances, or sometimes for no apparent reason, and the trucks trundle Transvaal-wards only half full. Though, of course, what they do bring is all out-of-the-ocean fresh.

It can be argued that the trawled fish brought in by Sea Harvest and I&J is also out-of-the-ocean fresh, for it is all cleaned on board the trawlers, and either frozen immediately or packed on ice, sufficient to keep it unspoiled until it comes to rest on the fishmonger's slab. In effect, it means that the customer in Johannesburg or Pretoria can buy fish in exactly the same condition as the customer in Cape Town or Durban.

We hear plenty of gripes and complaints, though, even from people living at the coast. Recently, we drove along the Natal coast from north to south and back again, making enquiries. Hardly a fresh fish to be seen, either at fishmongers, hotels or restaurants. Everyone told us the same story – they couldn't buy fresh fish from the ski-boats, because they were all under contract to Irvin & Johnson!

It's the irregularity of supply of linefish in inland centres that has most restaurants confining their menu-lists to the regularly available fish, usually just kingklip and sole. Though it's not the only reason. Unfortunately, we South Africans are as unadventurous in our choice of fish dishes as we are in every other kind of restaurant fare. So, grilled kingklip and grilled sole are often the be-all and end-all of fish selection.

Hardly any restaurant offers skate, for instance, nor do house-wives buy it from the supermarket, even though it's one of the cheapest fishes on the market; delicious too, when grilled or fried, served with black butter and a handful of capers. Not only politically are we one of the world's more conservative nations!

The result is that good restaurants, when they are able to get hold of an interesting fish, are liable to offer it as a "plat du jour", a "special of the day".

Over the past few years, a phenomenon has arisen in South African restaurants. Customers have gone all "continental"! They've taken to squid in a big way although, of course, it's in-variably referred to as "calamari". Who knows, one of these days, perhaps, ordinary South African restaurants will be offering dishes of octopus, too.

The phenomenal growth of interest in fish in our restaurants is due partly to the increase in its availability, and partly to a marked move away from red meat. (In this country, that's a phe-nomenon indeed!) The trend is noticeable particularly at lunch-times, when business-folk appreciate the lightness of fish, mak-ing its ingestion easy and its digestion swift.

We decided to publish this book because all indications were that the public would like to see – and try for themselves – some of the fish dishes created by our professional chefs. We re-jected some of the recipes submitted to us, if they were too com-plicated, too thoroughly exotic for the average home-cook.

All recipes in the book, therefore, are practicable, workable by the ordinary cook, and fairly simple. Some need more time and trouble to assemble, some take two or three trips to the stove during the cooking. All are possible, though. Sometimes an in-gredient may be elusive, but substitutes can always be found.

As pointed out earlier, this is not your rigid culinary bible: it is meant to give you some ideas, some useful bits of information, perhaps – and even a smile here and there!

Standard recipes

In many of the recipes that follow, you will find items repeated, such as fish stock or fumet, fish velouté, sauce Hollandaise, court-bouillon, and so on. Rather than print the recipes for these each time they occur, here are some of the standard items which all chefs use:

COURT-BOUILLON
(an aromatic liquid in which meat, fish and some vegetables can be boiled.)

1. BASIC

1 large onion, unpeeled, sliced	1 carrot, sliced
1 leek, sliced (include some of the green)	1 stick celery, sliced, including a few leaves
6 pieces parsley, including stalk	small bunch thyme
6 pieces dill	1 bay leaf
300 mℓ dry white wine	1ℓ water
	10 black peppercorns

METHOD:
1. Place a pot with 1ℓ cold water on medium heat, then add all the above. Heat until boiling, then reduce heat and simmer for about 15 minutes, with the lid on.

2. Now pour in the dry white wine (some people prefer a smaller quantity) and bring to simmering heat again. Simmer for another 15 minutes.

3. For the last 10 minutes only, drop in the black peppercorns.

Note: Allow to cool. Pour into small containers, enough for 1 dish each. Cover well and the court-bouillon will keep fresh in the refrigerator for several days. If you make a good deal more, though, you can keep it for a long time in the freezer.

2. WITH VINEGAR
Use the same vegetable mixture as for the basic court-bouillon. Instead of white wine, however, use some red or white wine vinegar. DO NOT USE MALT VINEGAR. For 1ℓ of court-bouillon, 150 mℓ of vinegar should be enough.

3. MILK AND LEMON
Add one part milk to four parts water that has been lightly salted. Peel a lemon completely, carefully getting rid of every piece of the white, bitter, pithy part. Cut the lemon into very thin slices with the sharpest knife you own. Lever out any pips, and throw away. Use as much lemon as you want. You may cook this mixture beforehand, before you use it with fish, or if you prefer you can put the fish directly into the milk-and-lemon liquid without any prior cooking.

Sauces & dressings

ROUX

The roux is an essential basis for thickening sauces, the foundation on which sauces are usually built, both in the kitchen restaurant and at home. There are two kinds of roux: white and brown. They are made with the same ingredients to begin with, but change in character as heat is applied.

A mixture of flour and fat is blended gently over low heat, for five minutes or for a considerably longer period, depending on the colour you wish your roux to be. A white roux should not colour at all and becomes the basis for white sauces such as béchamel. Brown roux should reach the colour of a hazelnut and it should have a delicious baked smell.

It is most important to cook the roux long enough to dispel the raw taste of flour, otherwise that unpleasant flavour will dominate even the strongest spices, herbs and seasonings. Stir the flour and butter continuously to distribute the heat and allow the starch granules to swell evenly. This enables them to absorb the liquid properly and will result in a fine, smooth, creamy sauce.

FISH VELOUTÉ

(a fish stock added to a basic roux, with wine added)

60 g butter   **60 g flour**
250 ml fish stock   **250 ml dry white wine**

METHOD 1:
Make a roux from the butter and flour. Add the fish stock, stirring constantly, then add the white wine (as dry as possible). Bring to the boil and simmer for about 15 minutes.

METHOD 2:
Extra ingredients:
pinch sugar   **pinch cayenne pepper**
squeeze lemon juice   **dash cream**

Make a roux, as above, then add a very little sugar and some cayenne. Add white wine, lemon juice, the water in which you have boiled the fish, and cream. Bring to the boil until the sauce is thick enough.

BÉCHAMEL SAUCE
(a basic sauce that combines milk with a roux, and is the foundation of many others)

STANDARD BÉCHAMEL:

45 g butter	45 g flour
500 mℓ milk, heated but not	3 mℓ salt
boiling	a little nutmeg (if liked)
pinch pepper	

Make a roux. Add the milk slowly and mix well with a whisk until sauce thickens. Before sauce boils, reduce heat and simmer for a minute or two, stirring well with a whisk to prevent lumps forming. If you need to keep this sauce for a time, put some softened butter on a knife and pass it over the top. This will prevent skin from forming.

FLAVOURED BÉCHAMEL:
To the previous ingredients add:

1 small onion (skin on)	1 clove
1 bay leaf	2 slices carrot
mushroom stalks and	1 stick celery
peelings	

Bring to the boil, remove from heat, and allow to infuse for 1 hour before using. Strain and use as required.

There are different consistencies to a béchamel, according to requirements. If a thinner sauce is needed, simply reduce the quantities of butter and flour in the roux, but ALWAYS use them in equal quantities. Cream may be added to replace some of the milk, for a richer and heavier sauce.

SAUCE HOLLANDAISE
(an egg-and-lemon sauce that can be used hot or cold)

3 egg yolks	150 g butter
45 mℓ cold water	5 mℓ lemon juice
salt and pepper	pinch cayenne pepper

1. Melt the butter, which should only be lukewarm.
2. Place the egg yolks and water in a thick, shallow saucepan on a low heat, or in a basin over a pan of hot water. Take care that the water does not boil. Whisk until thick and foamy, remove from the heat, and beat in the melted butter a drop at a time, until emulsified. Now add the rest of the butter slowly, beating all the time.
3. Add lemon juice, season with salt, pepper and cayenne pepper, and keep lukewarm.
Note: If the Hollandaise should curdle, add about 20 mℓ boiling water and beat continuously until it becomes smooth again. If the sauce has to be kept for a time, add a little dry English mustard at the beginning, or a little béchamel: that will help to hold it.

FISH FUMET (STRONG FISH STOCK)

fish head, bones, trimmings (but not gills or viscera)
Same vegetables as for a court-bouillon
White wine

METHOD:

1. Place all ingredients in a pan. Cover with cold water. (It is better to chop up or break the heads and bones into small pieces.)

2. Bring the liquid to the boil, removing the scum that forms. Reduce the heat and allow to simmer gently for about 30 minutes. DO NOT ADD SALT. That is best added when you use the fumet in a recipe, after you have reduced it.

3. Place a colander or a wire strainer over a deep bowl and strain the fumet through it. It will be quicker if you press the solids down, but that will make the liquid cloudy. If you need the fumet for a clear sauce or an aspic, it is better to let the liquid seep gently through.

4. In order to get as clear a liquid as possible, strain again: this time through muslin or a fine sieve. Once again, do not press it, but allow to drip. Leave in the fridge for some hours, and the fine solids will settle at the bottom, as a sediment.

Note: For an aspic, add two or more fish heads, preferably line-fish. Their gelatine will give you a good quality aspic. Put into bakkies or strong bags; this can be deep-frozen. Before use, warm up and include bones and trimmings from the current fish you are using.

16

VEGETABLE STOCK

1ℓ water
2 celery sticks and leaves, chopped
1 onion, with skin, chopped
1 bay leaf
bouquet garni
2 carrots, chopped
1 turnip, chopped
1 bunch parsley with stalks
2 leeks, including some of the green
6 black peppercorns

Bring to the boil, simmer for 1 hour. Strain off the vegetables, reduce the liquid by one-half. Store in the deep-freeze.

Graça with langoustino's.

There are many ways to enjoy crisp white Graça.
With a handful of sardino's.
Or a lorryload of langoustino's.
The most rewarding way, however, is with a tableful of friendino's.
That way you get to share not just a refreshing taste, but also a sparkling experience.

Graça.
The talking,
eating, drinking,
laughing, singing,
sharing wine.

Produced in the Republic of South Africa.

MAYONNAISE

(for those without a blender or processor)

2 egg yolks	**3 mℓ dry mustard**
pinch pepper	**500 mℓ olive oil or salad oil**
15 mℓ vinegar or lemon juice	(the more oil you use, the
5 mℓ salt	thicker the mayonnaise will
	be)

Put all ingredients except the oil in a small basin, preferably a heavy one. Stir vigorously with a wire whisk. Add the oil, drop by drop. It is important that the oil should be at room temperature. When the first half is blended, the oil can be added more quickly. Use more vinegar or lemon juice, or a little boiled water, to thin the mixture, if required. Mayonnaise may be stored in the fridge if it is in an airproof container.

SAUCE MORNAY

(a very popular sauce for fish dishes)

60 g butter	**60 g grated parmesan or**
60 g flour	**gruyère cheese, or**
500 mℓ milk	**120 g cheddar cheese**
2 egg yolks	

Make a roux. Add the milk and stir continuously until boiling. Reduce heat and simmer for 5 to 10 minutes. Add the grated cheese, stirring all the time. Beat the egg yolks and the cream in a bowl, just enough to mix them. Take the sauce right off the heat – this is vitally important – and then add the cream and egg mixture. Stir with a wooden spoon. Re-heat very gently, but do not allow to boil.

Note: Over-beating or over-heating will make your sauce elastic-like.

LOBSTER (OR CRAYFISH) SAUCE

1,5 kg cooked crayfish, or a good deal more crayfish heads and claws	**500 g tomatoes, skinned, de-seeded and chopped**
30 mℓ tomato purée	**3 chopped shallots (or small unpeeled onions)**
30 mℓ brandy	**30 mℓ butter**
15 mℓ oil	**1 stock cube, chicken or vegetable**
6 parsley stalks, chopped finely	**1 clove garlic, crushed**
10 mℓ dried tarragon or 30 mℓ fresh, chopped	**pinch cayenne**
250 mℓ white wine	**salt and pepper to taste**

METHOD:

Crush the lobster heads and claws with a rolling pin. Heat the oil and butter, add the shallots (or onion) and garlic. Put in the crayfish and flare with the brandy. Add the white wine and simmer a little. Add the chopped tomato and tomato purée. Season with salt, pepper and cayenne pepper and add the stock cube. Simmer for 20 minutes.

Strain and return the liquid to saucepan. Add the parsley and a little tarragon. Thicken with beurre manié (*see below*), adding small pieces at a time until the sauce is at the required thickness. Bring to the boil once or twice.

Beurre manié: Knead together butter and flour in the proportion of about 2:1, but the butter may be reduced in quantity to about equal with the flour. Keep in fridge in plastic bag for further use. Break off small pieces when using.

TOMATO AND FISH SAUCE
(a good substitute for crayfish sauce)

120 g butter
1 clove garlic, crushed
1 small onion, unpeeled,
  sliced
1 sprig of thyme

120 g flour
120 ml tomato purée
1 bay leaf
750 ml fish stock

METHOD:
1. Melt the butter in a pan, add the onion and garlic. Sauté until golden-brown, then add the flour and let it simmer for a few minutes, stirring all the time.

2. Add the fish stock, tomato purée, bay leaf and thyme. Simmer for half an hour, stirring occasionally.

3. Remove from the heat. Strain or liquidise.

Note: This sauce can be kept in the fridge for 2 or 3 days. It can be laced with brandy or cream before serving and it is a very useful stand-by when crayfish are not available, or too costly.

SAUCE TARTARE
250 ml mayonnaise
30 ml chopped gherkins

30 ml chopped parsley
30 ml chopped capers

Add chopped parsley, gherkins and capers to the mayonnaise, and stir.

MAITRE D'HOTEL BUTTER
(a garnish for fish or meat dishes)

120 g butter
salt and pepper
juice of ½ lemon
20 mℓ chopped parsley

Soften the butter, then add the parsley, lemon juice, salt and pepper. Put this in foil and make into a roll about 2 cm to 3 cm thick. Put in the refrigerator to harden and cut into slices as required.

GARLIC BUTTER

250 g slightly salted butter
2 cloves garlic, well-crushed
60 mℓ chopped parsley
30 g finely chopped shallot
  or onion
pepper to taste

Mash well together.

LOBSTER BUTTER
(crayfish butter)

the creamy intestine of the
  crayfish and the roe
30 g unsalted butter
30 g flour

Put all together and mix with a fork. This is used to thicken and add more colour to a crayfish dish.

CREME FRAICHE

100 mℓ buttermilk
500 mℓ thick cream

Mix thoroughly. Stand for 24 hours at room temperature.

SEAFOOD COCKTAIL DRESSING

100 ml home-made mayon-
  naise (or Hellmans, the best
  of the commercial brands)
10 mℓ creamed horseradish
5 mℓ dry English mustard
5 mℓ Worcester sauce
dash of Japanese "mirin" or
  dry sherry

Mix the mustard and Worcester sauce first, then mix all together.

You can make this sauce pink, if you like, by adding tomato ketchup or even a smidgeon of cochineal or rose-pink vegetable dressing.

BEATEN BUTTER

Several recipes call for the addition of beaten butter. Here's a simple way of preparing it: Cut up about 125 g butter with a kitchen knife. Keep the chunks small. Spread them on a plate and keep them in the refrigerator to chill. In the meantime, bring the same amount of water (just a tiny bit more than 125 mℓ) to a boil over a high heat. As it boils, begin to add the chilled butter, piece by piece, beating vigorously. Add a little salt (especially if you are using unsalted butter) and a squeeze of lemon juice. Keep the sauce warm, either on a barely-heated stove, or in a bain-marie – a bowl immersed in a pan of hot water.

HOW TO SKIN AND DE-SEED A GREEN OR RED PEPPER

Place the peppers in a hot oven for a few minutes until the skin begins to bubble. Remove, skin, discard the inner pith and seeds.

Alternatively, drop the peppers in a pan of very hot oil for a few seconds only. This will loosen the skin and make peeling very easy.

Mussels, clams and oysters

There is a good deal of fear, mostly justified, about eating mussels that have been casually plucked off the rocks around our coasts. Every year, people become ill and some even die from contaminated mussels. The risk is small, but why take it at all?

If you must eat mussels locally, consult the locals. If they are eating mussels happily, so can you. There are two main sources of contamination: oil slicks and the notorious "red tides". Oil is pretty apparent and everyone affected will know about it. Look out for oily, scummy, grey-to-black discoloration of the beach and rocks.

Red tide is the common term for the phenomenon of a certain kind of dead plankton that is washed shorewards. Only one in five red tides is toxic, and its approach canot be forecast. When the thickest part of the red tide reaches the beach, it shows on the surface of the water and looks almost like canned tomato soup. It is spongy and can be lifted out of the water and pressed between the hands (though doing this is not advised, either).

It affects shell-fish life wherever it appears and renders it poisonous, too. However – and here lies the greatest danger – the trouble with the toxic red tide is that it is highly poisonous long before it is concentrated enough to become visible! A careless person could die before the first red-coloured water became apparent. The answer is, therefore, in case of doubt – don't!

There is an absolutely safe source of mussels, however, these days. It is the west coast port of Saldanha, where an enterprising marine biologist, Philip Steyn, has built up a flourishing business called West Coast Maricult, and where he breeds mussels and clams, under the brand-name "Seafarm". His shellfish come with a guarantee that they are absolutely free from all the major causes of shellfish contamination, and their standard is always maintained by a team of experts.

So successful has this farm become that today it is shipping out over four tonnes of shellfish weekly, properly selected, well-packed and insulated against long journeys. Those are the only fresh mussels guaranteed to be completely safe in South African waters.

Clams are seldom seen wild around our coasts in large quantities, but Seafarm cultivates them very successfully, as well. Everything that applies to mussels applies to clams as well, and those from Saldanha are delicious.

The only other sources of mussels and clams you can rely on are the imported varieties: frozen, canned, in brine, etc. They're all right as a stand-by, but nothing beats the taste of a really fresh shellfish.

Oysters come from a number of sources in South Africa. They are gathered wild all round the coast but, again, it is the cultivators who can be absolutely relied upon. Oyster farming was pioneered by the Knysna people, who are still big suppliers. There is a fine oyster farm just outside Port Elizabeth, called Hougham Park Oysters, which has grown considerably these past two or three years. Both these enterprises grow mainly the British Colchester and Whitstable type of oyster.

Now, though, in Swakopmund in Namibia, a South West African entrepreneur named Timo Voges is very successfully breeding an oyster never seen in South Africa before: the Pacific or Japanese oyster, and by all accounts they are marvellous shellfish. This type of oyster, it is said, has become the most-consumed in the world and is the favourite of European connoisseurs.

Cultivated oysters tend to have smaller shells than their wild cousins, but more or less regular in shape and size. Wild oysters sometimes have huge shells, in weird shapes and sizes, sometimes in contrast to the flesh within them. There are other differences between the cultivated and the wild fish that the consumer should be aware of. Cultivated oysters have a life of several days out of the water, provided they are handled carefully, kept cool, preferably covered in seaweed and dampened, or in a refrigerator.

Never, in any circumstances, keep live oysters in a bucket or a sink of water. Oysters stay alive for days and, like all living creatures, they have to breathe. They do this by slightly releasing the firm grip between the two halves of their shells, exuding water in which they have released carbon dioxide, and taking in water from their surroundings, from which they obtain oxygen. If there is no water around them, they gradually lose all their own water and die of oxygen starvation. If they exude their carbon dioxide into a small, enclosed, surrounding body of water, though, they breathe that same water back in . . . complete with the poisonous carbon dioxide they have breathed out. Then they breathe it out again, and in again, so polluting their own water, and they die even more quickly and turn the water rotten.

Cultivated oysters that have been in the fridge for a day or two should stay tightly closed. If they are slightly open, the careful man would not want to eat them raw, on the half-shell, but usually they are perfectly suitable for cooking. The heat of the cookery process would kill off most of the bacteria. You have to be very careful with wild oysters, however. Their "shelf-life" is

usually far less than that of cultivated oysters, mainly because of their ungainly, thick and irregularly shaped shells.

If they could be packed flat, with the join between the half-shells horizontal, their life would be longer. Packed carelessly, at all angles, their liquid tends to seep out faster, and they will die, often within 24 hours of leaving the sea. Because of their erratic shape, though, they usually have to be packed in sacks, every which way up. We prefer the cultivated variety, therefore, unless we are eating wild ones fresh from the sea, at the coast.

Then, you can often come across a bad 'un in a batch shipped by careless hands. You probably won't realise it, though, until you've eaten it. Even at the seashore, if you are gathering these most delicious of all shellfish, be sure to take them off the rocks. Do not gather any that are loose in the sea, with no seaweed attached to them. They will have been torn loose from their mooring by the tide, "tumbled" ashore, perhaps left on dry land for a tide or two in the hot sun, returned to the sea, revived a little by the water, but undoubtedly in a deteriorated condition, then tumbled ashore again.

The small boys who usually gather wild oysters for the market have been told, of course, to leave those oysters strictly alone, but at 10c a fish they are sometimes inclined to take chances. If you are in a restaurant, therefore, that sells wild oysters, you should be safe with those that have some seaweed or marine growth attached to their shells. Those that haven't might possibly have been tumbled ashore and the vegetation worn off them by successive tides. And do not, under any circumstances, eat wild oysters whose shells are open. Ask the waiters to show the shells first, before you decide to order them.

COOKING RULES
All very simple. With mussels and clams, do not attempt to cook any that are open, whereas an oyster is usually safe to cook even if it is slightly ajar (as long as it has been kept refrigerated); though not if well-opened. After a few minutes exposure to boiling water or steam, all mussels and clams will open. Those that don't, chuck away without another thought.

Overcooking of all shellfish will usually toughen them. Undercooking is always best. The cooking process will generally continue while the fish are kept warm.

If you open mussels or clams in a mixture of ingredients necessary to your recipe, the liquid from them will naturally be utilised. If you open them in steam or boiling water, do not discard the liquid that gathers in the pan. Reduce the boiling water drastically, and combine the liquid with your reserved fish fumet or stock.

When opening oysters, use either a proper "shuck", that you can buy at good hardware or kitchen stores, or a strong, short-bladed knife, something like a hunting-knife. Wear a glove in your left hand, or wrap your hand in part of a cloth, and open the fish over a basin. Rest your elbow on the table, and your wrist on the rim of the basin. Hold the oyster firmly, and insert the point of the knife into the place where the two halves of the shell join. Wiggle the point about until you sever the muscle. Now, before opening the shell, push the knife farther in, against the inner surface of the bottom shell, and sever the muscle that joins the flesh to the surface. Now open the shell, trying to retain as much of the liquid as you can, but allowing the spill-over to drop into the basin.

If you remove the top half of the shell, the oyster should now be ready to be served on the half-shell, or the flesh removed for use in a recipe. The liquid in your basin is valuable. It is full of taste and nutrient. Strain it through a cloth, to get rid of bits of splintered shell or sand. Add it to your food wherever it can be used, or remove it very fast to the refrigerator, and later on to a container to be deep-frozen.

If you should get enough of this liquid, though, add a touch of lemon-juice to it, plus a smidgeon of Worcester Sauce, and drink it as a cocktail. It's marvellous!

Condiments and spices

SALT

Keep it dry, of course, otherwise you'll have pouring problems. Unless the recipe specifies otherwise, try not to add salt to the food until the last possible moment. Salt is extremely persistent. Even in the deep-freeze, after all other condiments have weakened, salt stays salty.

Too much salt early in the preparation of a dish can ruin it. With a stock, particularly, of meat, fish or vegetables it is best not to use salt at all. Wait until the stock is finished and drastically reduced: then add only a minimum. The time to use the salt is when the stock is incorporated into your recipe.

PEPPER

Nearly every recipe calls for "freshly ground pepper", and that is certainly the best. It is not always easy to have a pepper mill in the kitchen, because of the dampness. Pepper kept airtight for a week is still within the description "fresh". Grind enough for a few days, therefore, and keep it in one of those opaque, plastic medicine-containers every household seems to collect.

Even for the table, freshly ground salt and pepper are nicest. There are some pretty fancy salt and pepper mills in the shops costing a fortune. There are also some small, wooden, utility, sensible models. Keep two: one for black pepper (which is unri-pened) and one for white (which is the stronger, mature pepper).

SPICES

Every home keeps a few spices. If they are ground, they won't have a useful life in your kitchen of more than a few weeks. If they are whole, they will last longer. That attractive spice-rack on the wall, though, is not the best place for them. Keep small quantities only on view: keep the rest deep-frozen in the recesses of your freezer.

We know very many home cooks who like to put spices, whole or ground, into a frying-pan before use, heat them until the kitchen is redolent of the aromas of the East, and only then pop them into the food to be cooked. This is not sensible. The tastes and aromas of spices are carried within them in their essential oils. If heated, the oils give up their characteristics, and little is left for the cooking.

Take the spices off the shelf, however (or, even better, straight out of the deep-freeze), grind them or use them whole, and mix them with whatever food you are cooking, and the essential oils will release their tastes and aromas inside the food, which is where you want them.

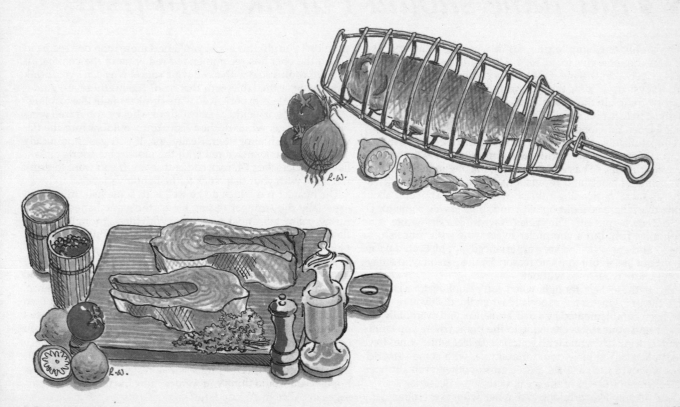

What wine should I drink with fish?

There's only one, simple rule: drink whatever wine you like. And it's the same rule for all food. There are lots of people who don't – yet – drink wine at the table because they are sometimes put off by fears of doing the "wrong thing". Believe us, there is no "wrong thing". In the words of good old Marie Lloyd, the queen of the English music-hall 80 years ago, "A Little of What Yer Fancy Does Yer Good"!

Unfortunately, as interest in drinking the excellent wines of South Africa has spread from the upper-crust few to the ordinary folk like us, so has wine snobbery, the phenomenon of people drinking labels and reputations instead of the wine itself. There's more misleading rubbish written (and spoken!) about wine than there is about politics, and that's saying something!

So don't be put off. The "rules" say drink a dry white wine with most fish. But if you prefer sweet wine with your fish, go ahead and enjoy it. The very experienced, sophisticated palate might not like it, but that's no reason for the person who enjoys sweet white wine to go without.

One of these days, though, when you're looking for a change, give the dry wines a try, especially when the dish you're eating has been complemented by a delicate sauce, and eventually you might find your tastes changing to the point where you'll only want to drink dry white with your fish. Sweet white wines have their place at the table, too: for example, with some very rich hors d'oeuvre such as pâté de foie gras or other, even stronger, pâtés; and at the end of the meal, with some desserts.

And if you like drinking red wine with everything, why shouldn't you? In this book, you'll find more than one recipe in which the chef has recommended red wine in the cooking. If you can cook a sole with a red wine sauce, why can't you drink a red wine at the table with that dish? Again, there are guidelines that the less-experienced wine-drinker might like to follow.

For instance, it would be silly to drink a heavy, robust red wine with a delicate, white-fleshed fish. You would swamp the flavour of the fish altogether. Really, too, it isn't gastronomically sensible to drink such a red with the more robust sorts of fish, like musselcracker, 74, rock cod and so on. If you want to drink red wine with your fish, stick to the lighter varieties.

The heavier red wines do go well with some fish, mind you, especially the stronger tasting kinds, the game fishes, such as tunny, yellowtail, snoek and so on. With these, though, a good, flavourful, heady white wine goes just as easily. But it's do as you please, though, all the way.

There's one aspect of wine-drinking where "do as you please" does not apply, though – by law! If you're dining in a fairly good French or Italian restaurant that has a Wine and Malt licence, they are not allowed to sell you a bottle of wine from their own country! The only restaurants that are permitted to sell imported wines, beers and spirits are those with a full licence, and if you could see the regulations laid down by the Liquor Board (every member of which, of course, and every inspector working for it, is a long-experienced, professional restaurateur . . . some hopes!) you would think you were reading the more lunatic passages in "Alice in Wonderland".

Continued on page 30 ➡

Daybreak at Nederburg, in the Paarl Valley.

Imagine a wine that captures the delicate copper-pink blush in a dawn sky and the crisp freshness of the new day.

Elegant. Intriguing. Unique.
A dry, cultivar wine, with a delectable herbiness,
an alluring aroma and a distinctive hue.

From the Winemasters.

Nederburg
Cabernet Sauvignon
Blanc de Noir

We'd like to share Nederburg with you.
Call us at (02211) 623104 to arrange your visit.

"Wine with Fish" from page 28.

Metric Measures

If you are not yet fully accustomed to metrication (which applies to the majority of us), here are some conversions. Because of the law of the land we are obliged to omit the old measurements in the text of the recipes.

1 cup	is now	250 mℓ (millilitres) (1 000 ml = 1 ℓ)
½ cup	is now	125 mℓ
1 tot	is now	15 mℓ
1 tablespoon	is now	15 mℓ
1 teaspoon	is now	5 mℓ
A standard winebottle contains		750 mℓ
1 lb (pound)	is now	454 g (grams) (1 000 g = 1 kg)
(1 kg is equivalent to		2,2 lb)

Herbs, when fresh, are measured in the recipes by weight in g. When chopped, and more easily measured in spoonsfuls, they are given in mℓ (eg: 10 mℓ = 2 teaspoons; 15 mℓ = 1 tablespoon).

Would you believe, for instance, that you can't buy a bottle of French wine in a restaurant that doesn't have three egg dishes on its menu? Or that hasn't carpets on the floor, even if that floor is antique, beautifully kept, yellow-wood timber? One of these days, when the powers-that-be manage to sort out our political and social problems, perhaps they'll devote a little time to changing the liquor laws of this country, to bring us up to the level of other civilised lands.

> **ALL THE RECIPES IN THIS BOOK ARE FOR FOUR PERSONS, UNLESS OTHERWISE STATED.**

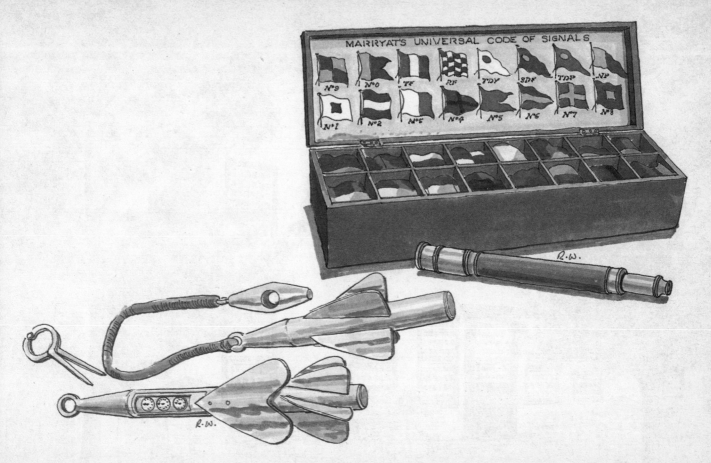

MARRYAT'S UNIVERSAL CODE OF SIGNALS

R.Ward '8?

Alphen Hotel ★★★ TYYY
Alphen Drive, Constantia 7848
Cape Town
Telephone: (021) 74-1011
PO Box 35, Constantia 7848
Open daily
Fully licensed

*A*lphen

An impressive piece of Cape history, a National Monument, a building of grace and charm set in its lush and peaceful gardens – yet a thoroughly modern hotel, beautifully furnished with valuable antiques, comfortable and cossetting, and offering some of the finest hotel dining-room food in all the Cape.

The Cloete family acquired Alphen in 1850 (it had been built a century before) and it was their family seat for another century. Turning this glorious place into a hotel was a recent development (by the standards of history, that is) and since it opened its doors to the travelling public, Alphen has become world-famous.

There's a highly professional kitchen, providing excellent meals, although the chef, Chris Greeff, is not overawed by the antiquity surrounding him. He has been impressed before, because in his imposing portfolio of culinary appointments was a spell at Buckingham Palace. You can't get grander than that!

His style of cooking is well in keeping with modern tastes and styles. Mr Greeff believes in lightness of touch but enough on the plate to satisfy even the very hungry. He is imaginative and innovative, and we are impressed with the recipes he has given us for this book.

As is to be expected, Alphen's wine-list includes many of the best marques of the Cape, together with several imported labels and, of course, several of their own wines.

Dining inside, in the "Agterkamer" or the "Heerenkamer", or on a summery day outside on the Terrace, can be a most relaxing and rewarding gastronomic experience. Alphen is truly lovely.

Alphen Red Roman with Fennel

INGREDIENTS:
4 red roman of 250g each, or 1 large
fish of 1 kg
4 fennel bulbs
2 shallots or 60 g chopped onion
breadcrumbs
2 large cloves garlic
60 g Parma ham, cut into strips (any
raw smoked ham will do)
a little olive oil or melted butter
salt, freshly ground black pepper

METHOD:
1. Scale and clean the fish. Do not remove head or tail.
2. Trim the fennel, reserving the leaves, and cut the bulbs into quarters. Chop them coarsely.
3. Chop the garlic, shallot or onion, and add the chopped fennel.
4. Cut the strips of ham into tiny pieces with a very sharp knife and mix into the fennel, shallot and garlic. You will now have an attractive mixture that the Italians call a "battuto".
5. Heat a little olive oil or butter in a shallow pan and put the battuto mixture into it. Cook gently until tender and juicy. Season to taste with salt and pepper.

6. Remove about half of this mixture to a bowl and mix in a few breadcrumbs. Stuff this into the cavities of the fish.
7. Brush the fish with oil and grill.
8. Serve on a bed of the reheated fennel mixture. Chop the reserved fennel leaves finely and scatter over the fish. Garnish with lemon.

ALTERNATIVELY:
The fish can be baked in the oven, then laid over the fennel mixture.

HILTON-RICHFIELD
Real Parma ham from Italy is not only hard to get, but impossibly expensive. Luckily, excellent local versions of prosciutto ham are made by several companies. Particularly good are those from Rietmann's in Cape Town and Taurus Meats in Johannesburg. Alphen's chef has been careful to point out that you need a very sharp knife to cut prosciutto ham into strips. Well he might — have you ever tried cutting raw smoked ham with a blunt knife?

34

Sole Alphen

INGREDIENTS:
4 fillets of sole, about 170 g each
1 bay leaf
3 or 4 peppercorns, black
150 mℓ cream
2 parsley stalks
½ onion, coarsely chopped
200 mℓ dry white wine
15 mℓ pear liqueur (or 15 mℓ pear juice
    plus 10 mℓ brandy)
salt, freshly ground black pepper
2 cooking pears, peeled, cored and
    halved (any green-skinned, medium
    sized pear will do)
Court-bouillon (see "Standard
    Recipes")

METHOD:
1. Warm the court-bouillon, if it has been made previously and stored. If freshly made, do not allow to get completely cold.
2. Season the court-bouillon with salt and pepper, if required, place the halved pears in it and poach until tender.
3. Lift out the pears and leave in cold water for a few minutes to refresh. Add the wine to the court-bouillon and leave it to cool.
4. Wrap each fillet of fish around a pear half, season lightly, and poach gently in the court-bouillon.
5. Lift out the fish and pears very carefully, and keep hot while you reduce the liquid to one-third of its original volume.
6. Add the cream and simmer for 10 minutes until the sauce reaches the consistency to coat the back of a wooden spoon. Add the pear liqueur (or the pear juice plus brandy). Taste and add salt and pepper if required.
7. Serve the fish and pear halves coated with the sauce. Garnish with twists of lemon.

> **HILTON-RICHFIELD**
> *Good to see pears in a fish recipe. Obviously the softer varieties won't stand up to this cooking method, gentle though it is. Readers who live far from the lush fruitlands should have no difficulty in finding the right kind of fruit.*

35

R. Ward '86

Kei Road, Bisho, Ciskei
Telephone: (0401) 9-1111
PO Box 1274, Bisho 5600
Open daily
Fully licensed

Amatola Sun

Of all the casino operations falling under the banner of Sun International, the Amatola Sun at Bisho, Ciskei's capital, is probably the most intimate.

It's not only a question of size (there are only 83 rooms), but of style and spirit. We have never seen a more dedicated bunch of people than the staff of this resort hotel. It seems as if they know they are out of the mainstream of their big brothers, Sun City and the Wild Coast Casino, and they want to make up for it with enthusiasm and super service.

Everything you expect of a resort is here, on a small scale, of course. Even the single dining-room seats only 120, so that chef Terry Manns has a clock-round job fitting in all the cooking, preparation, ordering, presentation and the hundred-and-one tasks involved in the serving of three meals a day – plus parties and special events!

The daunting complexity of his task only seems to fire Terry with more enthusiasm and inventiveness. He innovates. He surprises. He tempts. And he still finds time to give guests a sight of his excellent and artistic butter sculptures, for which he has won several awards.

So good is the food here, in fact, that at week-ends particularly the place packs out with local residents, who can find nothing of this quality in their own surroundings. We can understand it. The sheer professionalism of Terry Manns and his brigade would do credit to a downtown restaurant in a big city. See what this dedicated chef does with the fresh fish that comes up from the nearby coast daily, and you will see the work of a true artist of the kitchen.

You should not be too surprised by this. A few years ago, possibly, it might have been startling, but with the present policy of Sun International towards food being similar to that of the other large groups, we are all beginning to take excellence for granted.

Lattice of Trout with Champagne Sabayon

INGREDIENTS:
2 medium sized trout
1ℓ champagne
4 carrots, sliced
1 onion, sliced
squeeze lemon juice
1ℓ fish stock (see "Standard Recipes")
8 egg yolks
2 turnips, sliced
2 bay leaves
seasoning

METHOD:
1. Fillet two whole trout, giving four fillets.
2. With a very sharp knife, make 2 cuts from the head of the fillet down to the tail, leaving the three equally wide and long strips attached at the head.
3. Plait the three strips from the head to the tail, giving you a "koeksister" effect with the fish. Secure the end with a toothpick. (Once plaited and cooked in this way, fish retains its shape wonderfully.)
4. Now poach gently in simmering fish stock for approximately 3 minutes, adding lemon juice, salt and pepper, two bay leaves, sliced carrot, onion and turnip to the stock.
5. Remove the fish from the stock when cooked.

THE SABAYON:
6. Whisk 8 egg yolks together over gently boiling water. Slowly, bit by bit, add the champagne and fish stock in alternate drips. Keep whisking. The sauce should have the consistency of unwhipped cream.
7. Arrange the fillets of trout on to serving plates, and spoon a little sabayon alongside the plaited fillets. Serve with fresh garden vegetables.

HILTON-RICHFIELD
If you insist on using real champagne for this recipe, then make it Krug '76, which you can find here and there for about R100 a bottle. Let us know when you do this, and we'll come and help you polish it off. Alternatively, use Cape sparkling wine.

Sole Millefeuille with Red Wine Sauce

INGREDIENTS:
8 fillets of sole
400 mℓ fish stock (see "Standard
   Recipes")
400 mℓ reduced beef stock
4 egg yolks
dash lemon juice
2 shallots or onions, diced
2 turnips, sliced
2 carrots, sliced
salt and pepper to taste
200 mℓ red wine
400 g puff pastry
2 bunches watercress
2 leeks, sliced
15 g butter

METHOD:
1. Roll out the thawed puff pastry into a square of about 5 mm thickness.
2. Cut 4 rectangles measuring about 8 cm x 6 cm. Place on a greased baking tray. Brush with beaten egg yolks and bake in a moderately hot oven until golden brown. Remove from oven and allow to cool.
3. Cut pastry rectangles into halves horizontally.
4. Poach sole fillets in gently simmering fish stock. Add salt, pepper, lemon juice, sliced carrots, turnips and leeks to stock. Poach for approximately 3 minutes.
5. In another saucepan, put the beef stock and the red wine. Reduce for about 5 to 10 minutes.
6. Line each of the serving plates with the thickened stock.
8. Place one pastry base on each plate. Spoon some watercress on to each. Arrange two sole fillets on top of the watercress, and place thinly sliced cooked leeks on top of the fillets. Place the remaining pastry bases on top, as lids. Serve with fresh garden vegetables.

HILTON-RICHFIELD
If it seems a little incongruous to use red wine and beef stock with a fish as delicate as sole, try it for yourself and see how well it works. However, if we were to make any alteration to this excellent recipe, we would perhaps substitute a rich veal stock.

Landdrost Hotel ★ ★ ★ ★ ★ TYYY
Plein Street, Johannesburg
Telephone: (011) 28-1770
PO Box 11026, Johannesburg 2000
Open daily
Fully licensed

Barnato's

What a pleasant surprise it is to dine at Barnato's these days! Situated in one corner of the ground floor of the five-star Landdrost Hotel, on the very outskirts of the Golden City's central business district, many thought Barnato's would curl up and die, especially when the great and grand Johannesburg Sun & Towers opened up along the road.

On the contrary! To the surprise of all but the knowledgeable few, the Landdrost is flourishing. In fact, it is probably one of the most densely-occupied top-class hotels in the country. It is small, intimate, and serviced by a staff trained to the nth degree in the arts of making a guest feel truly at home.

Visitors to Johannesburg come back here time after time, feeling that they really belong. It is a heart-warming success story, particularly in view of the hard times our hotel industry is experiencing.

And Barnato's goes on and on. Its atmosphere of turn-of-the-century Joeys is as timeless as the mining-camp mementoes that decorate the walls. When Barney Barnato himself and Solly Joel and Cecil Rhodes and the Robinsons and all those colourful magnates were about, this is how they dined, one feels; in plush surroundings, attended by perceptive waiters, with satisfyingly-filled plates of properly-cooked, serious food.

There's nothing flibbertigibbet about Barnato's. It is a serious restaurant, and although there are one or two flights of fancy on the menu, for the most part the excellent produce is cooked to standard, classical, universally accepted recipes, as befits a five-star dining room. The rib of beef, of course, has been a favourite here since the room opened all those years ago. It's still the no. 1 best-seller and it takes a trencherman to finish it. But more and more people these days are going for fish – especially at lunchtime.

Salmon-Trout en Robe

INGREDIENTS:
8 slices salmon-trout, cut across
8 crêpes, about 160 mm diameter
100 g scallops
dash of Pernod
250 mℓ sauce Hollandaise (see
  "Standard Recipes")
5 mℓ tomato paste
50 mℓ eggwash (2 beaten eggs)
juice of 1 lemon
400 g puff pastry
1 bunch spinach, stems removed
60 g butter
250 mℓ cream
1 ripe tomato, blanched, peeled,
  seeded, chopped
8 new potatoes
salt and pepper
10 fresh mint leaves

METHOD:
1. Blanch spinach in boiling salt water. Remove to a colander; press out excess water; remove to dish and keep warm.
2. In a frying-pan, melt half the butter. Lightly salt it, and sauté the scallops. Remove and keep warm.
3. Melt rest of butter in a pan, add lemon juice. Cook the salmon-trout on both sides, about 2 minutes per side. Do not allow the fish to colour, or overcook.
4. Remove from pan and gently remove all bones and skin from the fish. Keep the fish in cutlet shapes.
5. Roll out the puff pastry (the pastry you buy in the supermarket is perfectly adequate) until about 5mm thick and twice the size of your salmon-trout slices.
6. Wrap the sliced scallops, the slices of fish and a portion of the cooked spinach, in each crêpe.
7. Wash the edges of the puff pastry with the beaten egg mixture.
8. Cover each crêpe in puff pastry and wash each with the beaten egg mixture.
9. Cook in oven at 160°C for about 12 to 15 minutes.
10. Serve with new potatoes boiled with mint leaves, and a sauce Choron (Sauce Hollandaise with the chopped tomato and a spoonful of tomato paste added to it).

PRESENTATION:
Serve on a fish platter, dress with new potatoes, sauce Choron served separately.

HILTON-RICHFIELD
The salmon trout from the western Cape coast is a good-looking and good-tasting fish, although it's really no more than a large rainbow trout, transplanted from fresh water to sea-water tanks and fed on pellets and crushed crayfish shells until its flesh turns pink. There is a difference in taste, though, after spending all that time in salt water, and it can make quite a spectacular dinner-table fish. This recipe, incidentally, isn't meant for bird-like eaters. It's a hefty dish, what with crêpes in pastry and all that rich filling.

Seafood Timbale Barnato's

INGREDIENTS:
1 sole, about 450 g to 500 g, cleaned, skin off, head and tail removed
2 large crayfish tails, poached, cut into medallions (ovals)
8 medium prawns, deveined, out of shell
100 g lobster butter (see "Standard Recipes")
250 mℓ fresh cream
500 mℓ good, strong lobster sauce (see "Standard Recipes")
100 g whole white button mushrooms
salt and pepper to taste
45 mℓ cognac
1 onion, chopped
200 g long grain rice
THE GARNISH:
100 g julienne of fennel bulb
100 g julienne of fresh white truffle

METHOD:
1. Fillet the sole. Cut each fillet into diagonal pieces (goujons).
2. Heat the lobster butter, and in it sauté the chopped onions and the mushrooms. Do not overcook. Now add the goujons of sole, the prawns and the crayfish medallions.
3. Add cognac to the fish, Cover with a lid and simmer for about 2 minutes.
4. Remove lid. Add the lobster sauce and cream.
5. Check the seasoning. Place in a mould and serve with white rice. Garnish with the julienne of fennel and truffle.

NOTE:
Chef John Gallagher warns not to cook the crayfish too much. It will finish cooking during the final preparation.

HILTON-RICHFIELD
Ready to run a mile at the thought of John Gallagher's julienne of fresh white truffle? You can import the real thing from northern Italy now and again, at something around R850 a kilo! Luckily, though, that isn't what John has in mind. There's a very interesting fungus from Namibia, arriving only occasionally, rather larger than the European truffle, and certainly one-hundredth of the price! Of course, it has only one-hundredth of the taste and the aroma, too. Ask your greengrocer if he knows about it. If it can be got (usually the hotels grab the lot as it comes in), use it. If not, use a julienne (very thin strips) made from the caps only of peeled, large brown mushrooms. And don't throw the stalks and the trimmings away — save them for a mushroomy sauce.

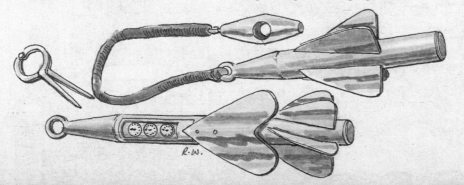

34a Cradock Avenue, corner Biermann Road,
Rosebank, Johannesburg
Telephone: (011) 788-3523
Open daily, lunch and dinner
Wine & Malt licence

Bone's

*B*one's is that fortunate thing in the catering business: an "in" restaurant. Built on the skeleton of the former Hot Tin Roof in Johannesburg's plush, upper-crust Rosebank, right next door to the splendid new auction rooms of Sotheby's, Bone's is a clever concept.

The ambience is smart and chic, but not the food. That is cleverly planned to be down-market and simple. Casseroles and stews, cooking "à la marmite" as the French put it, portions served in individual pots, stoneware and earthenware served at the table – all the little niceties of a country restaurant.

If you think this is all deceptively simple – well, yes, it is. There's a great deal of culinary skill gone into the planning and execution of the menus at Bone's. And there are no short cuts in the cooking that we have noticed. For instance, how easy it would be to produce sauces thickened the uncaring way, with cornflour or potato flour. Not in this kitchen!

Here, pan-juices are deglazed, thickened with cream and reduced the proper, classical way. An unexpected bonus in an operation of this nature, perhaps, but then the patrons of this restaurant are nearly all from the Smart Set, a fair number of whom would recognise the signs if gastronomic short cuts were taken in the kitchen.

David Varney, the owner of Bone's and of a chain of Italian restaurants as well, is a top professional. He knows how to make the iceberg above the waterline as attractive as possible, while below the surface the several levels of endeavour are controlled with rigid attention to detail. No wonder this restaurant is such a rip-roaring success.

Bone's Monkfish Mania

(a curried fish salad)

INGREDIENTS:
600 g cleaned and cooked monkfish or
   2 large crayfish tails
125 ml yoghurt or cottage cheese
200 ml pineapple pieces (fresh)
125 ml seedless raisins, chopped
10 ml Worcester sauce
5 ml parsley, chopped
pinch freshly ground black pepper
orange and lemon slices for garnish
500 ml cooked rice
1 small onion, chopped
4 dried peaches, soaked in a little
   water with 5 ml brandy
200 ml walnuts, chopped
5 ml medium curry powder
juice of quarter lemon
pinch salt
6 large cucumbers

METHOD:
1. Dice the fish, add to cooked rice and toss.
2. Blend the yoghurt or cheese with the pineapple, peaches, raisins, walnuts, onion, Worcester sauce, curry powder, black pepper, parsley, salt and lemon juice.
3. Chill cucumbers, slice off the top third lengthways, and scoop out flesh, to make a boat.
4. Add one-third of the blended mixture to the fish and rice mixture, and mix.
5. Fill cucumber boat with fish and rice mixture.
6. Pour balance of blended mixture over the fish and rice.
7. Serve cucumber boats on crushed ice and garnish with lemon and orange slices.

HILTON-RICHFIELD
Interesting choice here, between monkfish and crayfish. We know which we prefer but, towards the end of the month, in our usual impecunious state, we'd probably go for the monkfish! Our own preference, too, is for cottage cheese over yoghurt, as much for the consistency as for the taste.

Viddy Trout

INGREDIENTS:
4 medium trout
150 mℓ milk
5 mℓ salt
60 mℓ flour
pinch freshly ground black pepper
50 g slivered almonds
75 g green and black grapes, blanched, skinned, seeded and sliced
50 mℓ white wine
120 g butter
small pinch ground cinnamon

METHOD:
1. Soak trout in salted milk for 5 minutes. Remove, and dredge lightly in flour.
2. Fry 20 g slivered almonds in a very little butter, turning constantly, until browned. Remove; dry completely on a paper towel.
3. Mix cinnamon into the white wine, and soak the grapes and almonds in it for about 1 hour.
4. Melt 100 g butter in pan over medium heat. Fry fish for 6 minutes on each side. Remove and keep warm.
5. In a clean pan, melt remaining butter and fry remaining 30 g almonds until golden brown. Add marinated grapes and almonds, and the cinnamon-flavoured white wine . . . just enough to your taste.
6. Pour over the trout and serve on very hot plates.

HILTON-RICHFIELD
We're not sure where the name "Viddy Trout" comes from, but the recipe's viddy, viddy nice. We don't know, either, if we'd want to soak a fresh trout in milk before cooking, though many people recommend it. A frozen fish, undoubtedly, responds well to this treatment.

Corner Tyrwhitt and Cradock Avenues,
Rosebank, Johannesburg
Telephone: (011) 788-4883
Closed Saturday lunch and Sundays
Fully licensed

Bougainvilia

Professional chefs; that is, those whose training was academic in hotels schools in Europe, and who have been through the ropes as apprentices, juniors and sous-chefs, who have been shouted at and cursed in the steaming maelstrom that is the professional kitchen during a busy service; professional chefs by that definition have little time for the gifted amateur.

It's true that anyone who can cook a little thinks it's a piece of cake to open a restaurant. Most of them soon find out differently. Truth is, though, that there are many excellent restaurants in South Africa run by men and women who have never had a lesson in their lives.

Supreme among them we would place brilliant, creative, innovative Colin Steyn, lately of Pot Luck in Braamfontein, and now chef-patron of Bougainvilia in Rosebank, Johannesburg. Mr Steyn is most certainly not academically trained in the ways of the kitchen. But he has paid many a visit to France, and has watched and worked in several of the kitchens of the great restaurants.

His technical knowledge is as good as any hotel-school trained man, and his imagination and flair have brought him to the uppermost rungs of the culinary ladder in his country.

Here at Bougainvilia, in this chic and elegant room, the menu is almost entirely French cuisine and seldom departs from it. It is as close as anyone will get to "haute cuisine française" in this country. Mr Steyn's creations are always most acceptable, even when he juxtaposes two seemingly loggerheaded products on the plate. His sauces are beyond criticism: they are always sublime. He is undoubtedly one of the finest cooks in the land.

To meet the demands of the times, Colin has brought his prices within the reach of the ordinary man-in-the-street – provided, of course, that the man-in-the-street appreciates superb cooking. This doesn't mean the lowering of standards in any particular dish. It merely means that he plans his menus these days using rather less caviare, pâté de foie gras and fresh truffles . . . !

49

Trout Mousse with Tarragon Mayonnaise

INGREDIENTS:
500 g trout, filleted, skin removed, cut in chunks and placed in refrigerator at least 1 hour before needed. Must be very cold
250 mℓ crème fraîche or heavy cream (usually only to be found at Woolworths)
few gratings nutmeg
crushed ice
English cucumber slices
3 mℓ freshly ground black pepper
2 egg whites
10 mℓ brandy
5 mℓ saffron threads, soaked in a little water
hot water
salt to taste (about 5 mℓ)

METHOD:
1. Process trout in a food processor until creamy. Add egg whites with machine running. Add salt, pepper, brandy, saffron and nutmeg.
2. Place in a bowl on top of another which contains crushed ice. Refrigerate for half-an-hour.
3. Remove from fridge and slowly fold in the cream.
4. Butter a mould large enough to contain the mixture. Place the mould in a pan containing hot water (bain-marie). Bake in oven in the bain-marie until firm, about 30 to 45 minutes.
5. Remove from oven and allow to rest in cool place (but do not refrigerate) until it reaches room temperature.
6. Unmould. Decorate with thin cucumber slices. Serve with tarragon mayonnaise.

TARRAGON MAYONNAISE:
INGREDIENTS:
30 mℓ Dijon mustard
250 mℓ oil
3 mℓ lemon juice
60 mℓ whipped cream
3 egg yolks
15 mℓ tarragon vinegar
60 mℓ fresh tarragon leaves (or tarragon packed in vinegar, well-washed)
salt and freshly ground black pepper

METHOD:
Place mustard, egg yolks, salt and pepper in bowl of mixer. At high speed, beat for 1 minute. Turn mixer speed to medium, and slowly dribble the oil on to yolk mixture until thick. Add vinegar and lemon juice. Add chopped tarragon. Fold in whipped cream.

HILTON-RICHFIELD
Terrines, mousses and pâtés are always admired and enjoyed in restaurants, but so many home cooks find the prospect of making them a little daunting. A pity — it's really quite simple as long as all the preparation materials are carefully assembled before starting.

Fillets of Sole with Shrimps and Vegetables

INGREDIENTS: STAGE 1
90 mℓ unsalted butter
250 mℓ spinach leaves, cooked, drained, squeezed dry, roughly chopped
10 mℓ fresh dill, chopped
750 mℓ young leeks, washed and sliced
250 mℓ fresh sorrel, cooked, drained, squeezed dry, roughly chopped
salt and pepper to taste

METHOD:
1. Pre-heat oven to 180°C.
2. Heat half the butter in a saucepan, add leeks, season with salt and pepper, cook until wilted, but not soft.
3. In another pan, heat remaining butter until nut brown. Add spinach and sorrel. Heat through. Add this mixture to the leek mixture (above). Add dill. Stir to combine. Check for seasoning then remove all to a baking dish. Keep hot.

INGREDIENTS: STAGE 2
8 fillets of sole (2 whole large fish)
250 mℓ dry vermouth or white wine
toothpicks
salt and black pepper to taste

METHOD:
1. Butter another baking dish. Sprinkle the fillets of sole with salt and black pepper. Roll up tightly from tail. Insert toothpick to hold. Place them snugly in the dish. Pour vermouth (or white wine) over the fish. Cover with foil. Bake in preheated oven at 180°C for 15 minutes. Remove with slotted spoon.
2. Cut each rolled fillet in half and remove the toothpicks (the fish should now hold together). Arrange neatly over the vegetables you put into a baking dish (at step 3, Stage 1), the cut side upwards. Reserve the liquid the fish has cooked in.

INGREDIENTS: STAGE 3
Juice of 2 lemons
30 mℓ double cream (Woolworths keep it)
250 mℓ fish stock (see "Standard Recipes") plus sole trimmings
250 g soft butter

METHOD:
Place lemon juice in a saucepan. Boil and reduce to 30 mℓ. Add fish stock and the reserved sole liquid. Reduce to a glaze. Stir in double cream. Remove from heat. Add butter, slowly, whisking all the time. Keep warm over hot (but not boiling) water.

INGREDIENTS: STAGE 4
30 mℓ oil
45 mℓ brandy
750 g large shrimps, shelled and deveined
salt and black pepper to taste

METHOD:
1. Heat oil in pan. Add shrimp. Cook stirring until the shrimps turn opaque. Add brandy, and flame.
2. Spoon the shrimp over the sole in a gratin dish. Cover with foil. Place in oven until heated through, about 5 minutes. Spoon sauce over the top. Place under grill for 30 seconds. Serve at once.

NOTE:
Serves 4 as a main course, 8 as a first course.

HILTON-RICHFIELD

Colin Steyn, in this superb recipe, calls for unsalted butter, as most good cooks do. Have you noticed that when the price of butter comes down in a promotion, whether of a single store group or through the Dairy Board, the reductions only apply to salted butter? The reasons they give are always stupefyingly idiotic! Put it to the authorities that they are discriminating against gourmets and unlucky folk on a salt-free diet, and they do a Civil Service shoulder-shrug. It is iniquitous not to include pure butter in the price-reductions and we wish the consumer people would take this point up strongly.

Hotel Braamfontein ★★★★ TYYY
120 De Korte Street,
Braamfontein, Johannesburg
Telephone: (011) 725-4110
PO Box 32278, Braamfontein 2017
Closed Saturday lunch and Sundays
Fully licensed

Butlers

What a handsome room this is! It is not so large that you lose sight of the other side of it, and not small enough to be called intimate. It is, in fact, the ideal size for a top hotel's à la carte dining-room. Beautifully furnished and appointed, Butler's is quite as grand as any five-star room in the land. (The Hotel Braamfontein is a four-star establishment.)

There are two other drawcards here. One is master-chef Eric de Jonge, a Hollander who has travelled and worked at top restaurants all over the world (there are very few Nederlander chefs in South Africa, come to think of it), whose touch in the kitchen is unerringly correct. The other is Stefan Klein, the food and beverage director of the Hotel Braamfontein, who is dedicated to the concept of providing really top-class fare in his beautiful restaurant and who, in his limited spare time, also serves on the Transvaal Committee of the Chaîne des Rôtisseurs.

Between them, these gentlemen have succeeded in creating a dining-out venue of great refinement, a fact that is receiving growing attention from the cognoscenti of Johannesburg and the small but steady stream of overseas visitors to the hotel.

It is interesting to note that only a few years ago a hotel dining-room of this quality in South Africa would have been a brave gesture and nothing more. How our tastes have improved!

Butlers, in fact, must surely be counted among the better restaurants of the Transvaal.

Marinated Salmon with Honey and Mustard Sauce

NOTE:
This is enough for 10 people, but it's not worth making in smaller quantities.

INGREDIENTS:
½ side fresh salmon
2 bunches fresh dill, chopped
VEGETABLE MIXTURE:
3 medium carrots, chopped finely
1 stick celery, chopped finely
3 fennel bulbs, chopped finely
2 leeks, chopped finely
3 medium onions, chopped finely
SAUCE:
75 g honey
50 g French mustard
75 mℓ oil
20 g fresh dill, chopped
SALT MIXTURE:
(Must be prepared one week in advance)
1 kg coarse salt
75 g juniper berries
3 g black peppercorns, ground
10 g mustard seed
6 g dried rosemary
6 g dried thyme
75 g fresh coriander
5 g whole cloves
3 g bay leaves

4 g dried sage
6 g dried marjoram
grated skin of 3 lemons

METHOD:
1. Pull the salmon side through the salt mixture and lay it on a tray. Cover completely with chopped vegetables.
2. Place the dish of salmon, salt mixture and chopped vegetables, uncovered, in the fridge, for a minimum of 48 hours.
3. Scrape the vegetable mixture off the fish with a knife edge. Cover the salmon totally with chopped dill. Once again, place in refrigerator and leave for 48 hours.
4. Remove the dill. Slice the salmon very thinly, as you would a smoked salmon. Serve it not too cold (otherwise it will have no taste).

SAUCE:
Mix the honey and French mustard well. Slowly stir in the oil and finally add the chopped dill. Serve at the side of the sliced fish.

HILTON-RICHFIELD
Hardly the sort of dish you can knock up in a hurry when you have unexpected guests! A most original combination of tastes, though, and well worth the trouble. It's a kind of gravad laks, of course, but sweetish because of the honey. If you feel you can afford it, by all means use half a side of imported Canadian salmon. If you can't afford it, buy it just the same and starve for a month. Remember, though, that Cape salmon works splendidly in all these marinating recipes. Juniper berries are usually obtainable at good groceries or delicatessens. If they're a problem, leave them out.

Fillet of Sole "Picasso"

INGREDIENTS:
8 fillets of sole, about 100 g each
1 orange, peeled, pips removed, sliced
1 peach, sliced
40 g preserved ginger
50 g flour
juice ½ lemon
50 g butter
1 banana, sliced (don't forget to
   sprinkle a little lemon juice on it to
   keep the colour)
½ pineapple, peeled and sliced
25 g browned flaked almonds
45 ml dry white wine
salt and pepper to taste

METHOD:
1. Season the sole fillets and dredge with flour.
2. Fry them in a little butter until golden-brown.
3. Remove from the pan, shake off the butter, and dress them on four serving plates.
4. Place all fruit (except the banana) into the hot butter and stir slowly for 2 or 3 minutes. Add ginger.
5. Add the white wine to the pan, and the lemon juice.
6. Finally add the sliced bananas, toss a few times, and dress over the sole fillets, which you will have kept warm.
7. Garnish the dish with flaked almonds.

HILTON-RICHFIELD
Of course, you could make your own crystallised ginger, that pungent root being one of the few commodities that's quite cheap these days. But it's a long and painstaking job. Rather splurge out and get a jar of the real thing from your nearest Chinese shop: the better supermarkets carry it, too.

Please remember that the laws of the land forbid us to tell you how many spoonfuls go to make 45 mℓ. However, if you take a tablespoon and dip it into a cup of white wine three times, that ought to be enough.

R.W.

Casa Manuel

108 Corlett Drive,
Birnam, Johannesburg 2193
Telephone: (011) 440-5267
Closed Mondays
Wine & Malt licence

*W*hen Manuel Flores opened his little Spanish restaurant on Corlett Drive in Johannesburg's northern suburbs a few years ago, the knowing ones said it wouldn't last. There weren't enough people here, they said, to appreciate the cooking of that exotic land.

Wrong! Not only is Manuel still there, but he has doubled the size of his premises. And his is only one of three Spanish restaurants in Johannesburg. Who would ever have believed it possible? However, the popularity of paella and the zooming interest in zarzuela can be attributed directly to Casa Manuel, the excellence of its food and the rip-roaring, out-going effervescence of its owner's personality.

Of course Manuel sells more plates of paella than of anything else. But have some of his marvellous serrano ham, that smoked, raw delight from the mountains of Spain, as a starter. Try a plate of his unbelievably wonderful tripe, done in the madrileno way, and you will think it not just a plate of offal, but a sublime dish fit for the King of Spain himself. There are customers who come here regularly once or twice a month, who will seldom order anything other than Manuel's tripe – apart, of course, from his legendary fish dishes.

It's the enterprise and persistence of restaurateurs such as Senor Flores who are fast making Johannesburg a truly international gastronomic city. More power to them, and a jubilant "Olé" to the Casa Manuel.

Zarzuela

the classic Catalan seafood casserole

INGREDIENTS:
8 fresh clams
4 medium langoustines
1 crab (or few pieces)
500 g filleted kingklip, cubed
8 fresh mussels
12 small prawns, peeled, deveined
   (leave tails on)
2 crayfish tails
2 bay leaves
1 medium onion, chopped
250 mℓ dry white wine
dash brandy
1 big onion, sliced
30 mℓ olive oil
3 mℓ saffron threads
1 clove garlic, crushed
chopped parsley for garnish
2 lemons, for garnish
salt and freshly ground black pepper
   to taste

METHOD:
1. Place kingklip and all seafood in pot
with enough cold water to cover. Add onion slices, bay leaves, salt and pepper to
taste, and simmer for 5 minutes.

2. In another pot, heat olive oil, add
chopped onion, fry until just golden.
Slowly add water from simmering fish;
keep simmering. Add saffron. (If insuffi-
cient to turn stock yellow, add a thread or
two more.)
3. Now place all the fish into the pot with
the frying onions, add wine and if necessary add a little more water, to cover the
fish just barely. Add brandy. Simmer for
5 minutes.
4. Serve in a very hot soup plate. Garnish with chopped parsley and half a lemon per plate.

NOTE:
There are many variations possible. For
example substitute, or add, small oysters, sliced scallops, and/or pieces of
Spanish serrano ham or other smoked
prosciutto ham.

> ### *HILTON-RICHFIELD*
> *This dish should never be cooked in
> advance. It only takes 20 minutes to
> cook, if all the ingredients have been
> assembled and made ready. This
> recipe is simpler than the complicated
> casserole of north-eastern Spain. As
> Manuel Flores says, any of the
> ingredients can be substituted, or
> added to, according to availability.*

Kingklip, Catalan Style

INGREDIENTS:
2 kg kingklip, skinned, on the bone,
    cut into pieces 2 cm wide
250 mℓ oil for frying
THE SAUCE:
4 fresh clams
16 peeled shrimps
4 fresh mussels
handful of calamari rings
30 mℓ olive oil
8 capers
juice ½ lemon
2 bay leaves
250 g salted butter
8 black olives
2 fresh ripe tomatoes, skinned and
    chopped
250 mℓ flour
salt and pepper to taste

METHOD:
1. Season kingklip pieces well with salt
and pepper, then shake in a bag of flour.
Remove, shake off excess flour.
2. Heat oil in pan and fry fish pieces,
about 5 minutes each side, or until
golden-brown.
3. Take a clean oven pan, place fish in it,
sprinkle with lemon juice to flavour, then
cook a little more at 180°C for about 10
minutes. Use a fork to test when done
(the fork should pierce fish easily).

THE SAUCE:
4. Place olive oil in a pan with the butter.
Melt together on a low heat. Put in the
mussels and clams in their shells, and
the shrimps. Add the tomatoes, bay
leaves, olives and capers. Cook sharply
for 5 minutes. Test the calamari for softness (be careful not to overcook, as the
calamari will toughen).
5. Take fish from the oven, place on
warmed serving platter, and either pour
the sauce over it, or serve separately.

NOTE:
Some people (says Manuel) like the
sauce just as it is, without the fish. In that
case, pour it over slices of bread.

HILTON-RICHFIELD
We like Manuel's injunction to take a
"handful of calamari rings".
Everyone talked of handfuls
(handsful?) before modern cooks
reduced everything in the kitchen to
computer-like organisation and
precision. Interesting about calamari
– if you deep-fry it, do it fast, no
longer than 16 seconds. If you pan-
fry, cook fiercely for no longer than 1
minute. In a stew or casserole
situation, though, up to 15 minutes
cooking should not toughen the fish.
Don't ever cook this dish in advance:
it should be served right off the stove.
And save your precious olive oil for
this one. Any lesser oil just won't
taste right.
   Incidentally, don't confuse squid
with baby octopus: they're not the
same fish at all. Octopus is stronger-
tasting and tougher and requires a
different approach. The squid has ten
tentacles. Does this mean the octopus
has eight eightacles?

Champers

*U*nquestionably, one of the finest restaurants in the Cape.

You have to look for it, though, for it's tucked away in a tiny shopping area of Vredehoek, beneath the foothills of Table Mountain. But the journey will be well worthwhile.

Charming Norma looks after the room, while Hans presides over the ovens. That phrase, though, is far too banal to describe the quality of the dishes that come from his kitchen.

Hans Heidrich is German, a much-travelled chef and restaurateur who learned his profession in some of the greatest kitchens in the world. He served for a time as No. 2 in the famous Peninsula Hotel of Hong Kong; still the queen of the Kowloon waterfront. There the kitchens have to provide a variety of cuisines, all to the perfection expected of a great hostelry. Haute cuisine française, grills to American tastes, Chinese and Japanese food of several types; all poured from the Peninsula's stoves under the direction of Hans Heidrich.

He also practised his talents at the Hotel Souvretta, St. Moritz, at the Palace Hotel, Gstaad in Switzerland and aboard the m/s Kungsholm, the Swedish luxury passenger liner.

Classical French cuisine is his first love, however, as it is with most chefs of distinction in the western world. Heidrich is a master of the discipline. His sauces are outstandingly good: imaginative without going overboard with contrasts, based squarely on pan-juices and cream, reduced, reduced, reduced, until the very essence of the dish is captured. They equal those of any restaurant in the land.

Champers has a character all of its own – a delightful, flower-bedecked room, the walls dotted with a collection of historic menus from all over the world, some dating back to 1869. The table settings are impeccable, with elegant napery, crystal and silver ware. You will be most attentively looked after by Norma and her brigade, and you will enjoy some of the finest food in Cape Town.

Filets de Sole au Champagne "Brillat-Savarin"

INGREDIENTS:
16 medium sole fillets
50 g butter
150 mℓ fish velouté (see "Standard
   Recipes")
60 mℓ whipped cream
4 small vol-au-vent cases
75 mℓ lobster (crayfish) sauce (see
   "Standard Recipes")
300 mℓ dry white wine
30 mℓ finely chopped onion
75 mℓ champagne
150 mℓ Hollandaise sauce (see
   "Standard Recipes")
200 g shrimps, cooked and warmed

METHOD:
1. Melt butter in a pan, and add onions.
Place the fillets of sole on top of the onions. Add the white wine. Cover with foil
and poach gently until fillets are tender
(about 5 minutes) but still firm.
2. Remove fillets and keep them warm.
Add fish velouté to the poaching mixture
and cook, while stirring, until smooth
and slightly thickened.
3. While the mixture is still cooking,
whisk the cream briskly into it. Now
whisk in the champagne and cook for 2
minutes.

4. Warm the vol-au-vent cases in the
oven. Place them on serving plates. Fill
with cooked shrimps and top with hot
crayfish sauce.
5. Dress the cooked fillets of sole around
the pastry cases and top with the champagne sauce.
6. Place a small amount of sauce Hollandaise on each fillet. Serve immediately
with boiled potatoes.

HILTON-RICHFIELD
*Although this recipe calls for
"champagne", in true Champers
style, we believe anyone who can
afford to use genuine French
champagne in a recipe of this sort,
should also be able to afford a full-
time professional chef to cook for
them, so they wouldn't be needing
this book, anyway. Use ordinary
Cape sparkling wine (dry, cuvée
brut). We defy anyone but the most
sophisticated and experienced
professional gourmet to detect the
difference. When drinking, yes, but
in cooking, no!*

Oysters "St Tropez"

INGREDIENTS:
48 fresh oysters
60 mℓ onion, finely chopped
30 mℓ Pernod
pinch of dried thyme
50 g butter
freshly ground black pepper
8 medium tomatoes, blanched,
  skinned, deseeded and chopped
500 mℓ dry white wine
250 mℓ fresh cream
10 mℓ fresh dill, chopped
salt to taste

METHOD:
1. Open the oysters with a shuck, preferably over a basin so that you may keep all the liquid. Remove the flesh completely. Keep the better half-shell – usually the bottom half.
2. Warm butter in a pan. Sauté the tomatoes gently, then add the onion. Season with pepper, salt and thyme.
3. After a minute of two, remove from the heat, and spoon some of the mixture into each of the shells, giving 12 per person. Keep warm.
4. In another pan, pour in the white wine and the Pernod, and bring to the boil. Poach the oysters in this liquid for 1 minute.
5. Add the liquid obtained when opening the oysters to the pan, having first sieved it through muslin or cloth, allowing it to drip through. Boil the mixture until reduced by two-thirds.
6. Add the cream, and reduce by half again. Add fresh dill and salt to taste.
7. Spoon some of the sauce on to each oyster and serve.

> **HILTON-RICHFIELD**
> *Judging by the number of times Pernod appears in these recipes, it must be the favourite flavouring spirit of South African chefs, when cooking French fish dishes. It certainly adds a pungent, aniseedy flavour. Pernod is very similar to Ricard (in fact, Ricard bought the Pernod company a few years ago), but Ricard has a little more licorice in its taste. For our Greek friends, look no further than Ouzo — it's the same sort of thing.*

65

Sandton Sun Hotel ★ ★ ★ ★ ★ TYYY
5th Street, Sandown 2196
Telephone: (011) 783-8701
PO Box 784902, Sandton 2146
Closed Sundays and Saturday lunchtime
Fully licensed

Chapters

*T*he policy of Southern Sun Hotels of raising the standards of their à la carte dining facilities has been highly successful. It meant giving each hotel virtual autonomy in the planning of its menus and the styling of its culinary approach. It also meant bringing some top men into South Africa, men whose expertise and experience had already elevated them to positions of respect in the international catering world.

Such a man is Norbert Piffl, the splendid chef who was invited here to run the splended Sandton Sun Hotel. Mr Piffl was given his head in the creation of Chapters, the beautiful room that is the flagship of the Sandton Sun's several food and beverage points. Norbert Piffl's task in the huge hostelry was formidable, for he had to cook for all those eating and drinking outlets – and at the same time see that Chapters remained aloof in its smartness and splendour.

Together with other senior executives, the design and décor were planned. Together with a team of expert chefs, the kitchen was planned. Together with brilliant executives such as Billy Gallagher, who controls the entire Southern Sun restaurant operation, the wide-ranging menu was planned. And Chapters offered itself to the discerning Johannesburg and visiting public.

This room can take its place alongside the world's finest hotel à la carte dining-rooms. There is just the right balance of formality and friendliness, just the right contrast between standard international dishes and recipes of greater-than-ordinary interest, to make the whole thing work perfectly. And when the service was placed in the hands of one of the most experienced and popular maîtres d'hôtel in the business, Gianni Steffenini, the room's success was assured.

Ceviche of Scallops

(A classical South American fish dish, marinated in lime)

INGREDIENTS:
**8 king scallops with their coral, or 16
   small ones
1 large red pepper, sliced thinly
90 ml olive oil
fresh coriander leaves
4 limes (lemons will do)
1 red-skinned onion, sliced thinly
8 black peppercorns
salt to taste**

METHOD:
1. Defrost the scallops slowly. Slice them in half horizontally.
2. Cut 4 slices from one of the limes (or lemons) and reserve.
3. Squeeze the juice from the remaining limes (or lemons) into a bowl.
4. Mix in the olive oil, peppercorns and salt.
5. Add the scallops, onions and red pepper.
6. Keep in the refrigerator overnight.
7. Serve cold in small glass dishes and garnish with reserved lime slices and a few sprigs of fresh coriander. (Coriander left overnight in the fridge tends to blacken.)

> ### HILTON-RICHFIELD
>
> *Can you imagine what this would be like with fresh scallops? None in this part of the world, regretfully.* But the frozen scallops from the Great Barrier Reef of Australia are readily available and their taste comes up magically with fresh lime juice. There are also some fine frozen scallops from the Irish Sea, packed in North Wales. Mariner's Wharf in Hout Bay have them. If you can't find fresh limes at the local greengrocer, get your cousin in Natal to send you some. Worth noting, too, that you can substitute a quarter of the juice required with bottled lime juice. It'll do. Don't disregard this recipe if you can't get limes, though. Use lemons and add Rose's Lime Juice. (*Seafarm at Saldanha are experimenting with scallops, however, and if all goes well they should come on to the market in a season or two.)*

Sauté of Barracuda in Chervil Butter

INGREDIENTS:
**4 fillets of barracuda, about 180 g –
200 g each
1 bunch fresh chervil
250 mℓ dry white wine
2 tomatoes, peeled, seeded and
chopped
2 large shallots, or small onions, finely
chopped
a little extra lemon juice
12 fresh green asparagus spears
100 g unsalted butter
125 mℓ fresh cream
20 button onions
juice of 1 lemon
Cayenne pepper
pinch of sugar
salt to taste**

METHOD:
1. Scrape or peel the asparagus. Use only the top 5 cm. (Keep the rest for another dish.) Boil in plenty of salted water, with a little sugar and lemon juice. Do not overcook – the asparagus should emerge "al dente". Take out of the water and place into ice-water, to keep the colour.

2. In the same water, poach the button onions. Strain and reserve.
3. Chop most of the chervil finely, keeping some sprigs for garnish.
4. Butter a gratin-dish generously. Place the fillets of barracuda inside and strew with the chopped shallots. Season with salt and cayenne pepper, then sprinkle with lemon juice and white wine.
5. Cover the dish with foil and cook in moderate heat for 10 to 15 minutes. Do not overcook – the fish should still be firm to the touch. lift the fish out and keep warm, still covered with foil. The warming-drawer of your stove generally has enough heat.
6. Pour the cooking liquor out of the gratin-dish into a large saucepan and reduce by two-thirds.
7. Take the asparagus out of the ice water and strain.
8. Add the cream to the reduced sauce and reduce again until velvety smooth. Add the asparagus, button onions, finely chopped chervil and chopped tomatoes, then check seasoning.

TO SERVE:
Divide each fillet into 3, and arrange on your four serving plates. Pour the sauce over the fish and arrange the asparagus and button onions attractively on each plate. Garnish with the reseved chervil sprigs. Serve with parsley potatoes or créole rice.

HILTON-RICHFIELD
Barracuda isn't always available; more's the pity, for it's one of the best fish in our waters, both for eating and for catching. Fish you can substitute in this recipe are also a little scarce, especially up-country – musselcracker, (steenbras is another name for it), stumpnose, swordfish. Geelbek, yellowtail and Cape salmon also respond well to this recipe.

A few years ago, any recipe demanding "fresh chervil" would have been received with a loud, long chorus of "whatever's that?". These days, most of us know it's a delightful green herb, even though it's not often seen in the shops. All the more praise, then to Pam Cullinan on her herb farm near Pretoria, and other intrepid growers round the country, for the pioneering work they have done in acquainting South African housewives with the joys of herbs in the kitchen.

The correct way to cook fresh asparagus, by the way, is to tie the bunch up again (once the "grass" has been scraped and a cm or so cut off the bottom), and stand it up in a pot of boiling salted water with the tips above the water-line. That way, they don't get soggy. Not many professional chefs bother with this method — but every French housewife does.

Hotel Elizabeth ★ ★ ★ ★ ★ TYYY
La Roche Drive, Port Elizabeth 6001
Telephone: (041) 52-3720
PO Box 13100, Port Elizabeth 6000
Closed Sundays
Fully licensed

Club Orleans

*T*he five-star Hotel Elizabeth towers over the sea front, its luxury and comfort seemingly turning the blind eye to all talk of depression in Port Elizabeth.

And the queen of restaurants in this seaside industrial city is undoubtedly the Club Orleans.

Visiting businessmen who are used to a pampered life in top hotels throughout the world immediately recognise, in the Club Orleans, the sort of ambience, service, cooking and food presentation they find in other lands. For this is international grillroom fare of the highest rank.

The accent is on French cuisine, of course, as it is in all international dining-rooms, and although very little that's truly exotic is offered on the menu, there is a nod or two towards the famous créole dishes of Louisiana.

Under the Southern Sun Hotel group's policy of allowing each top restaurant to develop along its own lines, the Club Orleans has developed a personality of its own, unique in the country.

The improvement in the standard of this room is typical of the way hotel cooking has gained in stature these past few years.

It is a very fine restaurant and a tribute to Southern Sun's corporate food policy.

Stuffed River Trout "Seefelder Art"

INGREDIENTS:
4 deboned fresh trout
20 mℓ port
40 g celery
100 g butter
100 g finely sliced mushrooms
2 egg yolks
300 mℓ fresh cream
2 carrots

METHOD:
1. Slice all the vegetables into thin strips. Sauté this julienne in a little butter.
2. Add 50 mℓ fresh cream and the egg yolks. Mix well.
3. Fill the trout with this mixture.
4. Place the fish in an oven-proof dish with rest of cream and the port. Bake at 180°C until cooked (approximately 10 to 15 minutes).
5. Remove trout, lift off the skin, and keep warm.
6. Reduce the sauce and add rest of the butter in small pieces with a whisk.
7. Pour sauce over trout just before serving.

HILTON-RICHFIELD
Just a technical point of culinary terminology. We notice that some South African cook-books and recipes refer to the method known as "sauté", and say "sauté gently", or "sauté over a low heat". This is an incorrect use of the term. The famous French encyclopaedia LAROUSSE

GASTRONOMIQUE defines sauté as: "To cook over a strong heat in fat or oil, shaking the pan and making whatever is in it 'sauter', or jump, to keep it from sticking to the bottom." It follows, therefore, that you can't sauté gently. Never mind, as long as we all know what we mean . . . !

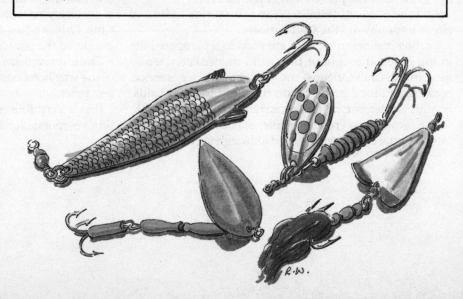

Hake with Walnut Sauce

NOTE:
Do not attempt this recipe with frozen fish. Only fresh hake will give you the taste. The sauce may be used with meat or chicken as well as with fish.

INGREDIENTS:
1 kg hake or merlu, cleaned and
   filleted
8 peppercorns
3 or 4 cloves garlic
5 ml ground coriander seeds
5 ml ground cinnamon
spring onions for garnish
2 bay leaves
100 g shelled walnuts
5 ml paprika
3 or 4 small onions, finely chopped
pinch ground cloves
90 ml vinegar or grape juice
fresh coriander (Chinese parsley,
   dhunia)
freshly ground black pepper
salt to taste

METHOD:
1. Cut the fish into portion-sized pieces. Put into a pan with the bayleaves, peppercorns and just enough salted water to cover. Simmer for 12 to 15 minutes.
2. Remove the fish from the pan and place on a serving dish. Leave the fish to cool and reserve the cooking liquid.
3. Pound the walnuts together with the garlic, paprika and salt to taste. Add the ground coriander seeds and mix well. Dilute this mixture to the consistency of single cream by adding some of the cooking liquid.
4. Pour this sauce into a pan, add the onions and simmer, uncovered, for 10 minutes.
5. Mix the cinnamon, cloves and pepper with the vinegar or grape juice, and add this mixture to the sauce. Continue to cook for 10 minutes more.
6. Pour the hot sauce over the fish. Leave to cool, then serve, decorated if desired with walnut halves, sprigs of fresh coriander and spring onion stalks.

HILTON-RICHFIELD

We are glad that one chef has recommended a recipe using hake, or merlu. It's a fine fish when absolutely fresh, but unfortunately it can taste like wet blotting paper when frozen and badly defrosted. This recipe is almost a Chinese dish. In fact, to give it even more of the tang of the Orient, we suggest you use only half the quantity of vinegar or grape juice, and add 45 ml of Chinese Oyster Sauce (every Chinese store has it in stock).

R. Ward '86

Hyde Park Corner,
Jan Smuts Avenue, Hyde Park,
Johannesburg 2196
Telephone: (011) 788-1284
PO Box 41083, Craighall 2024
Closed Sunday evenings and Mondays
Wine & Malt Licence

Cortina

Since the cost of dining-out became a factor that had to be watched in the lives of ordinary people all over South Africa, a host of restaurants of the lower-priced kind has sprung up in cities and in country towns, in all sorts of unexpected corners. Some of them are very good indeed; some are shockingly bad. All of them provide a filling meal at low cost.

The Cortina is not one of these upstart restaurants, though. It has had a couple of years in its lovely airy premises in the Hyde Park Corner shopping centre in northern Johannesburg, and before that it was the favourite trattoria of people who knew Italian food, in its tiny home in the centre of town.

This is a family concern all the way through. Pappa Carlo Adamo, a chemical engineer by profession, first put the brilliant cooking skills of his wife Ida to work years ago in town aided, when they could spare the time, by twin sons Paolo and Rafaello. It's a far bigger enterprise now. Carlo still presides over the room, and the delightful Ida, beloved of a generation of pasta-lovers, still helps the bri-gade to cook up a storm in the kitchen. Paolo looks after most of the cooking these days, though, but the size of the kitchen staff is warranted by the full tables in the big dining-room outside.

Rafaello spends most of his time running the family's ice-cream factory, Monte Cristallo, which supplies top-quality gelati to the trade throughout the Transvaal. And all the family muck in next door, helping the take-away pasta business to thrive. Hard work? You don't know what it is until you have seen the indefatigable Adamo family giving it stick. Of course, long hours, steamy conditions, pressures of service in a full dining-room, often create an atmosphere in which a good, honest explosion of Mediterranean temperament breaks out – but what do you expect in an Italian family trattoria, peace and quiet?

The food? Beautiful. Paolo Adamo has become a real expert, and his original creations are sometimes very admirable indeed. This is certainly one of the best Italian rooms in town.

Spaghetti alle Vongole

INGREDIENTS:
600 g spaghetti
250 g butter
2 cloves garlic, finely cut up
40 fresh clams (not frozen or canned)
chopped fresh parsley – plenty!
about 30 ml oil

METHOD:
1. Cook the spaghetti in plenty of boiling water for 10 minutes. (A little longer if you do not like your pasta "al dente".)
2. Remove the spaghetti from the water. Place in a large sieve and wash it well with cold running water until quite cold.
3. Place the spaghetti in a bowl and mix with oil, to stop the pasta from sticking together. Keep aside.
4. Wash the clams well. Discard any that show signs of opening.
5. Place the clams in a large shallow pan. Cut 250 g butter into largeish pieces and place them in the pan. Sprinkle lots of freshly cut parsley and add very finely cut up garlic. Cover the pan with its lid.
6. Cook very slowly. Do not allow the butter to burn. When the clams open they release their liquid. At this point, add the cold spaghetti. Increase the heat so that the spaghetti does its final cooking with the clams and the sauce.
7. When you see that the sauce has become very thick, serve in deep hot plates.

Do not use any kind of cheese with this dish – not even our marvellous Italian cheese!

> **HILTON-RICHFIELD**
> *Fresh clams are not always easy to find, but take Paolo Adamo's advice, and wait until you can buy some. Canned or frozen clams are a strict no-no for this dish. Clams that are alive hold a certain amount of tasty liquid, which adds a touch of sea freshness to the sauce. Wonderful clams are coming (too slowly for our liking) from Seafarm at Saldanha where those marvellous mussels are bred on ropes.*

Calamari alla Marinara

INGREDIENTS:
800 g calamari rings
2 bay leaves
2 cloves garlic, *cut*, not crushed
60 mℓ parsley, chopped, for garnish
600 g jam tomatoes (pomadori), fresh
   and very ripe, puréed (don't be put
   off if not available: use ripe ordinary
   tomatoes)
300 mℓ dry white wine
slices of fried bread
15 mℓ fresh oregano, chopped (or 30 mℓ
   dried)
salt and pepper to taste

METHOD:
1. Place the calamari rings in a large pot.
Pour over enough water to cover. Add a
little salt – not too much. Remember
that when the water evaporates, the salt
stays behind and your dish will be too
salty. Boil, with the lid off, until the water
is nearly all evaporated.
2. Pour in the white wine, add the
oregano, garlic and bay leaves and boil
for 10 minutes.
3. Add the puréed tomatoes and cook
until it all becomes very thick. Stir occasionally so that it doesn't stick and burn.
4. Serve in hot, deep plates. Sprinkle a
little cut parsley on top.
5. Serve slices of fried bread to accompany the soup.

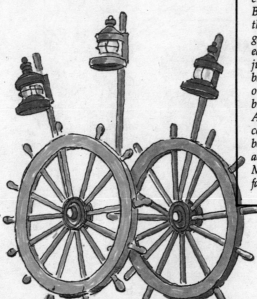

HILTON-RICHFIELD
*Notice that Paolo Adamo says you
should cut the garlic into slices; not
crush it. Fine, we go along with that.
But we like adding crushed garlic to
the bread when frying it for the
garnish. Fresh oregano isn't always
easy to get. Fresh marjoram will do
just as well or, failing that, fresh
basil. Do you say "oregano", like us,
or "origanum" as they write in the
brilliant Reader's Digest South
African Cookbook? The first is the
correct culinary term; the second the
botanical name. In both cases, the
accent falls on the second syllable.
Marjoram, incidentally, is the same
family and almost the same plant.*

79

45 Kruis Street,
corner Commissioner Street,
Johannesburg Central 2001
Telephone: (011) 23-8006
PO Box 864, Johannesburg 2000
Closed Sundays
Wine & Malt Licence

De Fistermann

*T*here are few enough specialist fish restaurants about. De Fistermann not only concentrates on fishy dishes (as its somewhat mysterious name implies – what language is it, exactly?) but the enterprising owner has hit on a formula that's a winner all the way.

This is a low-priced room – part à la carte, part help-yourself buffet – on the first floor of an office building in central Johannesburg. The great attraction is a cooked, hot, steaming, bubbling selection of fish stews and casseroles, plus an array of cold seafoods and salads, to which you help yourself – and go on helping yourself, to your heart's (or should that be your stomach's?) content – for an unbelievably low price.

We know of no other restaurant in which abalone (perlemoen) is offered in three different ways. Besides the usual fish dishes on the card there are some unusual ideas, such as a starter of mussels, shrimps and snails with a garlic sauce; a canneloni filled with shrimps, white fish, clams and spinach; a Cape Malay fish kebab; fresh snoek; a marvellous "potjiekos", that Cape Dutch favourite; and a fillet steak with smoked oysters (the only meat on the menu).

There's a big bar, too, with bar lunches at low, low prices, the dishes changing every day, with the half-dozen or so choices chalked up on a board. The service is by hard-working young women. It's not polished, of course, and the entire atmosphere is cheap and cheerful. And isn't that just right for the times?

Push your way in one lunchtime and try De Fistermann for yourself.

Fish Sosaties

(6 portions)

INGREDIENTS:

2 kg kingklip fillets, cut into 3 cm
  cubes
onions, cut into chunks
rice
200 g butter
2 green peppers, cut into 3 cm squares
bay leaves
sosatie sticks
100 mℓ oil

THE SAUCE:

200 mℓ fish stock (see "Standard
  Recipes")
10 mℓ curry powder
5 mℓ tomato paste
100 mℓ white wine
2 chopped onions
5 mℓ ground turmeric
250 g fruit chutney
200 mℓ oil

METHOD:

1. Thread on to sosatie stick 2 pieces of kingklip, then a piece of onion, a piece of green pepper, a bayleaf, then again 2 pieces of kingklip, etc., until stick is full. Allow two sticks per person.

2. Heat butter and oil together, and brown the fish on the sticks.

3. For the sauce, sauté onion in heated oil; add curry powder, turmeric and tomato paste.

4. Add fruit chutney and stir well. Add fish stock and white wine. Simmer for one hour. Check for seasoning.

5. At 15 minutes before serving, heat the sauce, place sosaties into sauce, and re-heat for about 10 minutes. Serve on a bed of rice and ladle sauce over sosatie sticks.

HILTON-RICHFIELD
Sate sticks (from the East Indies) are too small; wooden skewers are usually too big and clumsy. The proper sosatie sticks are just right. Best of all would be those marvellous kebab skewers in flat steel with ornamental handles, from Turkey and Iran and thereabouts — but when are we likely to see them again?

De Fistermann's Seafood Potjiekos

(For 6 to 8: not worth making for fewer)

INGREDIENTS:
1 kg calamari, with tentacles, cleaned,
   cut into rings 3 mm wide
350 g merlu, hake or kingklip, cut into
   3 cm cubes
1 x 500 g can mussels in the shell,
   drained
300 g butter
125 g button mushrooms, cleaned
45mℓ tomato paste
3 mℓ cayenne pepper
2 bay leaves
250 mℓ white wine
4 large carrots, cut into about 12 rings
   each
150 g medium size pickled onions
5 mℓ dried mixed herbs, or 30 mℓ fresh,
   chopped
pinch Aromat
300 mℓ fish stock (see "Standard
   Recipes")
3 large potatoes, cut into about 8 pieces
   each
salt and black pepper to taste

METHOD:
1. Sauté pickled onions in 200 g butter over low heat; add mushrooms and bay leaves. Add ground pepper to taste, then all the calamari.
2. Add herbs, cayenne pepper, Aromat, tomato paste and stir well. Cover with fish stock and white wine. Simmer for about half an hour, or until calamari is almost tender.
3. Add vegetables and simmer a further 10 minutes.
4. Lightly brown the fish in 100 g butter, then add it to the stew.
5. When fish is nearly cooked, add the mussels, take the pot off heat, allow the mussels to warm through. Check seasoning.

NOTE:
Prawns, crayfish, shrimps and langoustines may also be added. Use in or out of the shell (shell gives it a good flavour, though), chop the fish or leave them whole. Simply brown lightly in butter and/or oil before adding.

> **HILTON-RICHFIELD**
> *This is the first time we've seen a fish "potjiekos", and of course it differs in style and method from the traditional Cape "potjiekos" made with meats. This one tastes delicious: a sort of Johannesburg bouillabaisse.*

1st Floor, Marlborough House,
125 Fox Street, Johannesburg 2001
Telephone: (011) 331-3827
PO Box 2395, Johannesburg 2000
Closed Saturdays and Sundays
Fully licensed

Dentons

A combination of highly individual talents has made Dentons restaurant one of the most sought-after luncheon venues in Johannesburg. If people opted to come to the centre of town in the evenings again, Dentons would be just as packed for dinner.

Alan Gerson and his Belgian wife, Hélène, are the owners. Mr Gerson is well-known to the catering profession as one of the top wine experts in the country. His cellar is formidable; his selection of wines and spirits from around the world highly impressive. He has probably the most comprehensive range of ports, sherries, cognacs and cigars ever seen here.

His guided tastings are greatly appreciated by his customers. Gerson is more than just a local fundi, though: he is, as far as we know, the only South African to own a share in one of France's top vineyards, for he is part owner of the highly prestigious Puligny Montrachet estate in Burgundy. The splendid wine-rack at one end of the room is indicative of this restaurant's respect for wine.

When they decided to take over Dentons a few years ago, it was natural that Hélène, with her built-in Belgian flair for food, would supervise the kitchens. But the Gersons were fortunate in securing the services of a fine chef, Jonathan Montagu-Fitt.

Mr Montagu-Fitt is that rarity, a self-taught cook who has adapted to the rigorous demands of the professional kitchen. Even the academic purists, who insist that a chef can only be called that if he has done his three years at hotel school, admit that Jonathan cooks with style, panache, and a great deal of skill.

The style is French, of course, but dishes from other cuisines find their way on to the menu. There is no printed card, by the way: just a list of the day's dishes displayed on a couple of blackboards. This bistro-like announcement strikes the only discordant note in the room's pleasant décor, if the formality of the menu is important to you.

It shouldn't be, though. A list of dishes based on whatever is available at this morning's markets is the ideal way to ensure freshness, and the continual change which is the trademark of a really good restaurant of this type.

Kingklip Chinois

INGREDIENTS:
750 g filleted kingklip, cut into 16
  pieces the size and shape of fish
  fingers
1 small pineapple, 1 small fennel bulb,
  1 apple (preferably Granny Smith),
  all julienned into very thin strips
8 small white mushrooms, sliced
3 radishes, cut into rounds
2 large brinjals (eggplant)
6 strawberries, sliced

NB: Sprinkle all with lemon juice to
prevent discoloration, and keep well-
covered with plastic wrap.

oil for frying
30 m*l* flour

THE SAUCE:
600 m*l* water
125 m*l* white wine vinegar
100 m*l* pale dry sherry
1 piece root ginger 5 cm long, peeled
  and grated
50 m*l* sweet soya sauce such as Ketjap
  Benteng Manis
green sunflower or bean sprouts, for
  garnish
5 to 10 m*l* arrowroot or cornflour

70 g brown sugar
5 m*l* salt
a little oil for frying

METHOD:
1. Cut unpeeled eggplant lengthwise to
make 4 pieces, 2 cm thick. Salt and leave
to drain in a colander for 30 minutes.
Rinse, drain, and set aside.
2. Place all ingredients for sauce in pan
(except for arrowroot or cornflour). Simmer with lid on for 10 minutes, then
strain and remove ginger. Set aside.
3. When sauce cools, marinate fish in it
for 1 hour.
4. Wrap fish in foil and steam for 15 minutes.
5. Meanwhile, dredge brinjals with flour
and fry in oil. Drain and keep hot.
6. Heat sauce to boiling point, then add
5 to 10 m*l* arrowroot or cornflour
softened in water, and boil again for
1 minute. Add prepared fruit and vegetables and immediately remove from the
heat.
7. Place 1 slice hot brinjal on each plate
and over it 4 pieces of fish at intervals (if
possible). Pour on fruit and vegetable
sauce and garnish with green sprouts.

HILTON-RICHFIELD
*Jonathan Montagu-Fitt is one highly
motivated chef who always finds
interesting and exotic things to do. If
you have difficulty with the sweet
soy sauce (the Indonesian varieties
are becoming very dear), simply add
20 m*l* sugar to a full bottle of
ordinary soy sauce. Make sure,
though, that it's cooking soy you use.
The label on the bottle is usually clear
about its intended use.*

Roulade of Salmon

(Both salmon and sauce must be prepared 1 hour in advance)

INGREDIENTS:
8 escalopes of salmon (thin slices
    about 7 mm thick)
8 lettuce leaves (iceberg), blanched
juice of 1 large orange
10 mℓ lemon juice
5 mℓ salt
100 m cream
8 spinach leaves, blanched, stalks
    removed
400 g unsalted butter
40 mℓ gin
3 mℓ fresh white pepper
15 mℓ green peppercorns, drained
small cucumber balls rolled in
    chopped parsley, for garnish

METHOD:
1. Flatten the spinach and lettuce le
Place 4 salmon escalopes on spi
leaves, and 4 on lettuce leaves. Us
maining spinach and lettuce leav
cover them.
2. Roll them, making sure that the
tidy edges are underneath. Place
small cake rack, or any other rack

have (such as those that come with a pressure cooker) that will stand in a cooking pot. Pour boiling water into the pot first, then place the rack inside it: the water must not, of course, reach the level of the rack. Steam with tight lid for 10 minutes. Switch off, but leave lid on.
3. Meanwhile, soften the butter, beat it until white, then add orange juice, gin, lemon juice, pepper, salt, peppercorns, beating all the time. (NB. *Beat* not *blend!*)
4. Place hot salmon rolls on plates (1 of each per person) and heat sauce in pan with cream. Check seasoning and serve with the garnish of cucumber balls.

HILTON-RICHFIELD
Blanching is a very useful procedure for many fruits and vegetables. It's always tempting, though, to keep the greens in the boiling water a shade too long. Rather raw than ruined! Always refresh the vegetables, by removing them and plunging them into ice water.

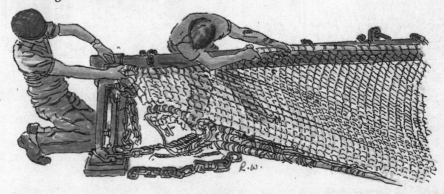

R. Ward '86

Somerset West Road,
Stellenbosch 7600
Telephone: (02231) 7-5079
PO Box 383, Stellenbosch 7600
Closed Sunday evenings and Mondays
Wine house licence

Doornbosch

*I*t's a joy to report the success of this restaurant, under the detailed supervision of Kurt Ammann – surely one of the country's most professional restaurateurs.

Mr Ammann owned and ran the famous Brixton TV Tower Restaurant in Johannesburg for many years, where his cooking, wine-list and five-star service brought him accolades from all parts of the world. Alas, he had to close down, for national security reasons, and Kurt decided to leave the Transvaal for the winelands of the Cape.

Today he owns the farm Rozendal next to the famous Lanzerac estate, and there he grows and makes some very good wine. A year or two ago, he took over Doornbosch from the KWV. It is one of the historical buildings of Stellenbosch (along the road to Somerset West), and it became a rather ordinary restaurant.

Now Kurt Ammann is chef-patron. He cooks, he services, he manages. And what glowing reports of his cuisine are reaching the rest of the country, where his former patrons smack their lips at the descriptions they hear of some of his dishes!

Ammann is Swiss, thoroughly immersed in the techniques and traditions of French cuisine (as are all good Swiss) but as thoroughly well-versed in the cooking of other regions, too. His menu is a short one, as is correct for a house of this type, but something of unusual interest will always be found on his list of "plats du jour". In fact, by far the major part of the Doornbosch menu is based on what's at its best in the local markets on any particular day.

On any list of top South African restaurants, Doornbosch must surely rank high.

Yellowtail aux Poivrons à la Doornbosch

INGREDIENTS:
4 slices of yellowtail about 200 g each, or 8 slices of 100 g
20 mℓ flour
½ red pepper, skinned and chopped into 5 mm squares (see method for skinning at end of "Standard Recipes")
½ green pepper, skinned and chopped into 5 mm squares
30 mℓ oil
125 mℓ cream
juice ½ lemon
500 mℓ fish stock (see "Standard Recipes")
200 g butter
½ red pepper, for blending
½ green pepper, for blending
fresh chervil
salt and pepper to taste

METHOD:
1. Reduce fish stock until only 125 mℓ is left.
2. Melt 170 g of butter gently. Place unchopped red and green pepper halves in blender with the reduced, still hot, fish stock, and blend for 2 minutes. Add the melted butter very slowly. Now you should have a thick, mayonnaise-like sauce.
3. Remove this sauce to a saucepan, add cream and the chopped pepper pieces. Season with salt, pepper and lemon juice. Warm through.
4. Prepare a plastic bag with seasoned flour. Shake the pieces of fish in the bag, making sure all surfaces are covered. Remove from bag and shake off excess flour.
5. Fry the fish in the remaining butter and oil on gentle heat until golden brown.
6. Pour the sauce on to a serving platter or individual plates. Place the fish in the centre. Decorate the fish with fresh chervil.

> **HILTON-RICHFIELD**
> *According to Kurt Ammann, whose word in the kitchen is The Law to us, monkfish (angler fish) can be substituted for yellowtail, but we should imagine any linefish will do. Notice Mr Ammann likes to spread his sauces at the bottom of the plate, putting the food on top. Very modern and very attractive!*

90

Darnes de Saumon au Pistou

INGREDIENTS:

8 slices of about 200 g each of fresh salmon, or slowly-defrosted frozen Canadian salmon, about 3 cm thick
36 leaves fresh basil, chopped
30 g butter plus a little extra
2 young onions, skinned until only the white part is showing
6 cloves garlic, chopped
90 mℓ olive oil
4 ripe tomatoes, blanched, peeled, seeded and quartered
100 mℓ water
100 mℓ fresh thyme, chopped
a little additional olive oil
salt, pepper, cayenne pepper to taste

METHOD:

1. Place garlic and basil together with the olive oil, salt to taste, and freshly-ground black pepper in a mortar, and grind them to a paste with a pestle. (Alternatively, drop everything into your fast mixter and liquidise.) This mixture is the "pistou", famous along the French Riviera.
2. Place a pot with the cold water on the stove, drop in the tomato and onion, and cook slowly until the tomatoes have dissolved.
3. Skin the salmon and cut the "darnes" (French for slices cut across) in halves. Oil an ovenproof dish with the rest of the olive oil. Season the darnes of salmon with salt, pepper and a little cayenne to taste. Arrange them in the ovenproof dish. Place a small roll of butter on each darne.
4. Pre-heat the oven to 200°C. Put the dish of salmon into the oven and cook for about 2 or 3 minutes only. Remove to the warming drawer, where it will continue to cook.
5. Reheat the tomatoes, add salt, pepper and cayenne pepper and the fresh thyme, bring to a swift boil and immediately remove.
6. The pistou can be served hot or cold. If it is to be served hot, heat it gently in a saucepan, stirring all the time.
7. Pour the tomato sauce on the serving plates and smooth it over the entire surface. Place the darnes of salmon (two per person) in the middle, and cover with the contrastingly coloured pistou.

NOTE:
If this dish is to be served cold (glorious on a hot summer's night), then do not oven-bake the salmon, but poach it in a court-bouillon (see "Standard Recipes").

HILTON-RICHFIELD
Canadian salmon, fresh or frozen, is pricing itself out of your reach and ours. Use fresh Cape salmon as an alternative. We find that in most recipes for real northern hemisphere salmon, the Cape variety (no relation, really) does very well. In gravad laks, for instance, Cape salmon is proving to be masterly. We suspect, too, that other Cape fish would respond to a pistou recipe. Try yellowtail, musselcracker, stumpnose, barracuda. They'll work just as well.

France

14a Plein Street
Johannesburg 2001
Telephone: (011) 834-7000
Closed Saturday lunch and Sundays
Fully licensed

Fisherman's Grotto

What are the factors that give a restaurant its character? The type of food, the quality of the cooking, the ambience of the room, the personalities of the management? Other factors, too?

Well, the Fisherman's Grotto is a phenomenon, for its success over the years rests squarely on two factors only: the utter magnificence of the cooking, and the larger-than-life personalities of Alan and Val Stricke. Alan is physically larger-than-life, too, while Val is petite. She seems too delicate to handle the heavy chores of the kitchen, but don't be fooled – she can be a tiger!

The room is nothing much: just a basement hollowed out with fish décor. The appointments are adequate. But, oh, the food! Val is arguably one of the finest cooks in the country, and her Japanese food has every Japanese visitor to these shores making for her door, so widespread is her fame.

Alan presides over the most remarkable cellars of wine, spirits, liqueurs, cordials and every other kind of drink you can name. It is probably the largest and most valuable in South Africa, and there are marques here, not just of wines you have never heard of, but even from places you have never heard of!

As far as fish is concerned, this is the spot if you want a guarantee of freshness. The Strickes own several ski-boats at the coast and fly the catches up three times a week. You couldn't do better than that at the coast itself.

There's no formality here. In the Fisherman's Grotto you become one of the family, so to speak, and you're liable to find Alan or Val pulling a chair up to your table and joining the party. If you consider this an invasion of your dignity and privacy, perhaps you'd better dine somewhere else.

If you are a real connoisseur of marvellous cooking, though, put aside all reservations about formal restaurant service, and indulge yourself down here in the Grotto. Most certainly, there is no better Japanese food anywhere in the world outside Japan – and the Japanese authorities say so themselves.

Mousse of Smoked Salmon and Trout

INGREDIENTS:
500 g smoked trout, filleted
500 g smoked salmon offcuts
500 g butter
rose-pink vegetable colouring
English cucumber, finely sliced
250 mℓ cream
black lumpfish caviar
several chives, chopped
THE SAUCE
125 mℓ creamed horseradish sauce,
  preferably the hot variety
ice cubes
125 mℓ cream

METHOD:
1. *Treat the trout and the salmon separately throughout.* Blend the smoked trout in your food processor. Remove and reserve. Cut the flesh of the salmon offcuts, and blend them.
2. Add 250 g softened butter to the trout mousse, mix gently, then pass through a sieve.
3. Add 250 g softened butter to the salmon mousse, mix gently, then pass through the cleaned sieve.
4. Put plenty of ice-cubes into a large bowl. Place a smaller bowl over the ice.

Put in the trout/butter mousse and beat in 125 g of the cream (which must be very cold) until smooth and fluffy. Remove, reserve: clean the smaller bowl.
5. Now place the salmon/butter mousse into the bowl over the ice, and again beat in 125 g of very cold cream. Add a drop of rose-pink colouring to the salmon mousse, as it tends to go a little brown after sieving.
6. Check for salt. There should be enough from the smoked fish. Take a glass mould and smooth the trout mousse into a layer over the bottom. Then layer the black lumpfish caviar over it equally. Finally smooth in the salmon mousse.
7. Refrigerate with a film or foil wrap for at least 24 hours, to set.
8. Turn out, slice and serve with creamy horseradish sauce.

THE SAUCE:
Mix the extra 125 g cream very gently with the creamed horseradish, so that it doesn't thicken too quickly.

SERVING:
Pour the sauce over your individual serving plates. Place a slice or two of the (now well-set) mousse on it, and garnish with a few very thin slices of English cucumber, with chopped chives.

HILTON-RICHFIELD
A lovely dish, not as wearisome to make as the length of the instructions might suggest, and it looks spectacular on the plate. Not cheap, either, and not for those with a cholesterol problem! You might remember to grease the inside of the mould slightly, with a film of oil, or of butter, or a whoosh of "Spray and Cook". Nothing more embarassing than making a beautiful terrine or mousse in a nice glass mould, and then having to smile wryly when the stuff sticks to the sides!

Clams with Chourizo

INGREDIENTS:
1 whole Portuguese chourizo
  (substitute Russians, if necessary)
1 bottle dry white wine
2 bayleaves
2 onions, coarsely chopped
½ to 3 chillies (see note below)
45 mℓ olive oil
2 kg washed clams
3 cloves garlic, crushed
salt if necessary and freshly ground
  black pepper
Fresh bread and butter and a green
  salad

METHOD:
1. Wash and rinse the clams several times. Discard any open ones.
2. Fry the chopped onion in olive oil (use green virgin olive oil for a stronger flavour).
3. Dice the chourizo sausage and add it to the onion for 2 or 3 minutes. Then add the bay leaves and the whole bottle of wine.
4. Bring to the boil, then add the clams. Simmer until all are open. This should take about 10 to 15 minutes.
5. Check for seasoning: sufficient salt should have come from the sausage. Stir in the crushed garlic and one or two chillies . . . watch their strength!
6. Just before serving, add freshly ground black pepper. Serve with fresh bread and a simple, green salad.

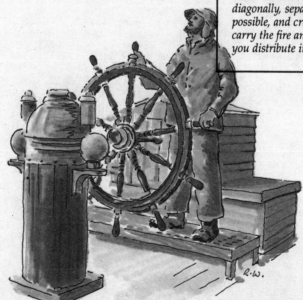

HILTON-RICHFIELD
Although Val Stricke recommends green virgin oil (and it's ideal for this, certainly), you might find the Cape olive oil, such as Costa's, suitably flavoured for this purpose. About chillies: always cut chillies diagonally, separate as many pips as possible, and crush. It's the pips that carry the fire and by crushing them you distribute it evenly.

R.W.

Capetonian Hotel ★★★★ TYYY
Pier Place, Foreshore,
Cape Town 8001
Telephone: (021) 21-1150
PO Box 6856, Cape Town 8000
Closed Sundays
Fully licensed

The Galley

*T*he dining-room of this flourishing 4-star hotel makes a special feature of its fish and seafood dishes, as its name implies. It's a dimly-lit room, with seafaring artefacts everywhere, and the lighting creates an ambience of intimacy that is very pleasant.

At the sides of the room, on two levels, pullman seating offers the diner almost complete privacy; the discreet ministrations of an excellent brigade of waiting staff add to his pleasure.

Of course, there is more than fish on the menu – no South African restaurant could survive without its grills and other meaty dishes. Here, in addition to the steaks, you will find mild lamb curry in the Malay style; as good a waterblommetjiebreedie as you could hope to find, and other typical dishes of the Cape.

Fresh mussels and clams from Saldanha come in regularly; fresh oysters from the finest farms; fresh fish of all kinds features prominently, all under the culinary supervision of Simon Eyre, a young chef from England, a thoroughgoing professional. He is typical of the new breed of British-trained chefs: dedicated, hard-working, motivated and, above all, displaying a degree of skill that will most certainly take him far.

This hotel is part of the Protea group, who are following the trend by upgrading the food in their dining-rooms throughout the land. This dynamic hotel chain had the inspiration of giving the group portfolio of food and beverage management to the brilliant William Stafford. Bill (everyone calls him that) won the coveted title of British Chef of the Year in 1982, and came to South Africa soon afterwards, where he lost no time in becoming a nationally known kitchen giant.

Stafford's influence on the chefs of South Africa in general has been significant, and on the dining-rooms of the Protea group it has been dramatic.

Perlemoen Soup

INGREDIENTS:
2 perlemoen
1,5 ℓ fish stock (see "Standard
   Recipes")
100 mℓ cream
50 g butter
whipped fresh cream
20 mℓ dark sherry
1 button onion, finely chopped
½ red fresh pimento, diced
pinch of fresh thyme
pinch paprika

METHOD:
1. Remove the perlemoen from its shell. Discard the black intestine and wash away any traces of black slimy film. Cut the perlemoen into small pieces and mince.
2. Heat the butter in a saucepan. Add the chopped onions and diced pimento. Cook for 2 minutes to soften. Add the minced perlemoen and cook gently together for 2 minutes.
3. Pour in the sherry and fish stock, add pinch of fresh thyme, bring to the boil and simmer for 5 minutes. Remove any impurities. Add cream and reduce slightly.
4. Season with salt and pepper to taste.

PRESENTATION:
Serve in a warm soup bowl. Stiffly whip the fresh cream and pipe it on to each plate of soup. Finally, sprinkle with paprika prior to serving.

HILTON-RICHFIELD
Fresh perlemoen are beginning to be seen occasionally inland. The shopkeepers are not too keen on stocking this delightful shellfish because they often get landed with the things, for perlemoen is another commodity that so many housewives turn their noses up at. Until recently, the only perlemoen available here was in tins, called "Abalone", imported from Hong Kong and Singapore, where they had been exported by the canners at Hermanus! The fresh red pimento called for here could be a bright red pepper, or forget the "fresh" and dice up a canned pimiento, preferably one from Spain.

98

Crayfish Fricassée "Capetonian"

INGREDIENTS:
4 x 600 g fresh crayfish
125 mℓ fish stock (see "Standard
   Recipes")
75 mℓ dry white wine
4 basil leaves, chopped
juice of ½ lemon
50 g cold butter (for the sauce)
125 mℓ cream
50 g butter
15 g fresh basil, chopped
30 mℓ brandy
1 tomato, blanched, peeled, seeded,
   chopped (keeping the pips and skins
   for stock)
a little oil
salt and pepper to taste

METHOD:
1. Remove crayfish heads and chop into
small pieces.

CRAYFISH STOCK:
2. Heat the oil in a saucepan, add all the
chopped crayfish heads and cook for 2
minutes. Add the tomato pips and skins,
fish stock and lemon juice. Bring to the
boil. Skim, then simmer for 20 minutes.
Strain.
3. Heat the butter in a saucepan. Add

the crayfish tails, fry for 2 minutes, then
add the crayfish stock. Bring to the boil
and simmer for 15 minutes.
4. Remove crayfish tails with a perforat-
ed spoon. Remove the crayfish meat
from the shells; slice it and keep on a
warm plate covered with damp kitchen
paper.
5. Boil the crayfish stock and reduce by
half. Add the cream to the reduced cooking stock, stir in the cold butter and add
the basil leaves and diced tomato. Check
the seasoning.

PRESENTATION:
Add the sliced crayfish to the sauce,
serve on a warm soup plate and garnish
with a fresh basil leaf.

HILTON-RICHFIELD
*When a recipe calls for butter to be
added to a sauce, always ensure that
it is refrigerator-cold. This slows
down the melting process and
improves the sauce. Butter for frying,
of course, can be any temperature.*

R-W.

8 Main Road, Melville 2092
Telephone: (011) 726-3602
Closed Saturday lunch
Wine & Malt licence

Gambarana's
(Freddies Tavern)

*T*he slogan this delightful little restaurant uses is "Not just a pretty place . . ." It's a good choice, for although the room is tiny, done out in shades of pink, with comfortable chairs and nicely-laid tables, the French (and sometimes a little Italian) cooking is of the highest possible standard.

Freddies Melville Tavern has nothing whatsoever to do with the other restaurants of the same name. So strongly is this felt that the owners have at last agreed to change their name to Gambarana's, which is a proud, three-generation Italian catering family name. Deo Gambarana is one of the doyens of the catering trade in South Africa and he is still found in his kitchens, supervising the production.

Assisting him is a clever Austrian chef, William Wallner, whose expertise and experience eminently qualify him for his job. The room is run by Errol Gambarana, (the third generation) with Paolo Sebastiani, who came from Italy 12 years ago and decided to stay.

This is not the place for fancy, intricate presentations. The cooking is simple and the dishes are offered to you simply, too. This food is to be eaten, not gazed at in admiration, although, of course, it looks thoroughly appetising. But what cooking! It is thoroughly professional but with a homely touch that so few other kitchens manage to achieve.

The wine list is not huge, but has some interesting labels to offer you, from some of the rarer and more rewarding estates in the Cape. This is Errol Gambarana's province, and how well he presides over it.

If you have an occasion to celebrate, where intimacy and personal attention seem to be called for, try Gambarana's.

Crayfish à la Turque

(By master chef Deo Gambarana)

INGREDIENTS:
4 raw crayfish tails
150 g butter
15 mℓ dry sherry
150 mℓ cream
a little flour
15 mℓ oil
5 mℓ paprika
15 mℓ brandy
salt and cayenne pepper to taste

METHOD:
1. Remove flesh from crayfish tails and cut in halves lengthwise.
2. Take 2 empty craytail shells and place in moderate oven. Leave until completely bone-dry. Remove and crush to a powder in a blender. (This can be a messy business, but persevere. If you haven't reduced the shells completely to dust, sift out the solids and discard them.)
3. Melt butter with paprika and crushed crayfish tail shells and cook gently for 2 minutes.
4. Lightly dust crayfish flesh with flour and fry in a little oil until slightly browned.

5. Warm the brandy (in a soupspoon is best), pour it over the tails and flambé. Add mixture from step 3.
6. Simmer gently until sauce thickens.
7. Season with salt and a pinch of cayenne pepper. Add sherry. Serve with savoury rice (yellow rice with chopped green peppers) or a mixture of brown rice and wild rice.

> **HILTON-RICHFIELD**
> *If you are lucky enough to be able to afford — or even to find — some wild rice, it goes magnificently with this recipe. Don't ever use it alone, though, and not only because of the high cost. Mix it in with brown unpolished rice for a truly remarkable side dish. Remember that the home cook can't flambé the way the restaurant waiter does. He has an open flame: you have to apply flame to the pan. Don't use a cigarette lighter, but a wooden match. If you have any doubts as to how the dish is taking shape when you come to the brandy bit, don't set light to it — drink it.*

102

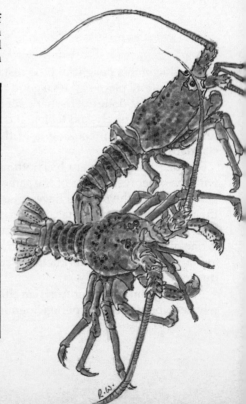

Kabeljou "Gambarana"

INGREDIENTS:
1,4 kg fresh kabeljou on the bone
1 ℓ fish stock (see "Standard Recipes")
4 sheets foil, 30 cm x 20 cm
4 green lemons
50 g cake flour
100 mℓ fresh cream
200 g vegetable julienne, made from
 carrot, leek, beans and celery
400 g butter
375 mℓ dry white wine
10 g fresh ginger root, grated
1 egg yolk (reseve the white for
 another use)

METHOD:
1. Clean and trim the kabeljou to make 4 steaks of approximately 200 g each.
2. Put the fishstock in a bowl, add the wine, and reduce by half.
3. Let the stock cool. Take half the quantity, put it into your freezer and leave until it becomes thoroughly jellified (about 2 hours). Keep the other half warm.
4. Melt 200 g butter in a saucepan and add 50 g cake flour. Cook gently for 3 minutes, then pour in the warm fish stock and cook gently until the mixture thickens. Now continue to cook on a low heat for ten minutes. Set aside.
5. Scrape the rind of one lemon. Squeeze the juice of the other 3 lemons into a bowl, and add the lemon rind, grated ginger, and the beaten egg yolk. Slowly stir in the fresh cream and set aside.
6. Place the kabeljou steaks on the pieces of foil. Place 50 g of the julienne of vegetables (must be very thin strips) on top of each fish steak equally, lengthways. Add 50 g butter and 15 mℓ of the fish jelly (from the freezer). Add salt and pepper, fold and secure carefully at the ends and side. Place in a pre-heated oven at 200°C (very hot) and bake for 15 minutes.
7. Warm up the stock (from step 4). While it is warming, pour mixture from step 5 into it, very slowly. *Important:* Do not allow to boil, as that will curdle the mixture. When all the mixture has been added, pour into a sauce bowl for separate serving.
8. Take steaks out of the oven. Remove carefully from foil and place on 4 separate platters (rather than plates), leaving the julienne strips in place. Serve with boiled baby potatoes or wild rice.

HILTON-RICHFIELD
The good home cook must get rid of prejudice against using fish heads. Get the fishmonger to cut or break a couple of heads up, and with some extra bones and skin add them to the fish stock you already have in your freezer or fridge. If you simply can't stand the sight, do it with your eyes closed. Nothing on earth will give you a fish aspic as tasty and as firm as that made with fish heads.

To take the rind off a lemon or orange, use the proper tool — a zester. All good kitchen shops have them, either with one cutting head or with 2 or 3. They take off just the fine outer thickness of the peel without pulling away any of the bitter pith.

R. Ward '86

Holiday Inn, ★★★ TYYY
Rivonia Road, Sandton 2199
Telephone: (011) 783-5262
PO Box 781743, Sandton 2146
Closed Saturday lunch and Sundays
Fully licensed

Grayston

*T*he Grayston is that incongruity, a five-star dining-room in a three-star hotel. It is the flagship restaurant of the Holiday Inn group, and it is without any doubt a splendid venue.

One man has made The Grayston what it is, the highly-respected Swiss chef, Heinz Brunner, backed by an expert and sympathetic management and a delighted head office.

Mr Brunner is not only a brilliant cook in his own right; his is a born kitchen administrator — so often even more important than simple culinary skills these days. But Heinz is also a sparkling cook in international competition. He was a member of the team of professional chefs who took part with such success at the Salon Culinaire International de Londres at Hotelympia in London in 1982; since then he has been the backbone of many a South African chef's team.

His latest accolade was given him in 1986, at the International Salon Culinaire in Johannesburg, when as Captain of the South African team he led them to a Gold Medal in the face of competition from some of the strongest cooking nations in the world, including the USA, Canada, Britain, France, West Germany, Spain, Portugal and Israel, who all sent teams to the Republic.

Of course, there is a world of difference between the food these great chefs create for international competition, and the dishes they serve every day from their kitchens. There isn't the time to perform these miracles in the commercial kitchen, and certainly no diner would want to pay the enormous prices that would have to be asked for them. It is comforting, though, to know that our chefs have the capability to rise to a splendid occasion, and are as good as their colleagues in any other country.

So, the food at the Grayston. It is excellent, naturally. It is very much to the taste of the guests who throng this pleasant room. It is international à la carte cooking at its very best. How could it fail to be with a chef of Brunner's calibre at the helm?

Crayfish "Isabel"

INGREDIENTS:
32 mussels
150 mℓ white wine
100 mℓ cream
16 balls from a spanspek melon
a little butter
½ red pepper, chopped
½ onion, chopped
200 mℓ fish stock (see "Standard Recipes")
16 balls from a honeydew melon
pinch curry powder

METHOD:
1. If using fresh mussels, scrub them, remove the beard. If using canned mussels, drain them, but reserve some of the liquid.
2. Sauté the onion in a little butter. Add the curry powder and the red pepper. Sauté for a minute or two, stirring constantly.
3. Add the mussels and cook for 2 to 3 minutes.
4. Add the white wine and fish stock and simmer gently for 5 minutes.
5. Add cream and stir well. Add a little of the mussel liquid and the melon balls. Cook for a further 2 to 3 minutes, stirring well. Season to taste.

HILTON-RICHFIELD

Chef Heinz Brunner says: "The sauce should be thin but if preferred it can be thickened with 'beurre manié', which is a mixture of softened butter and flour in equal quantities. Canned mussels can be used very successfully in this dish."

Chefs differ sometimes on the proportion of butter to flour in beurre manié. Master-chef Heinz Brunner is Captain of the South African professional team of gold-medal winning chefs. If he says half-and-half, so be it. It doesn't really make a bit of difference, because it's only a means of thickening a sauce quickly.

Mussels with Melon

INGREDIENTS:
4 crayfish tails
¾ medium onion, finely chopped
10 ml Pernod
pink peppercorns
a little butter
12 spears asparagus, fresh
140 ml fish stock (see "Standard
   Recipes")
125 ml fresh cream
250 ml cooked noodles
red caviar (for garnish – optional)
salt and pepper to taste

METHOD:
1. Cook the asparagus in boiling salted water until soft. Remove, drain, and blend in a food processor or liquidiser until it becomes a fine mousse.
2. Sauté the onion in a little butter until soft, but not brown.
3. Add the fish stock, the Pernod and cream, and reduce a little. If the sauce seems to be too thin, thicken with beurre manié (see previous recipe).
4. Fold the asparagus mousse into the sauce.
5. Steam the crayfish tails, taking care not to overcook.
6. Sauté the cooked noodles in a little butter until they are warmed through.
7. Coat the warmed serving-dish with the sauce and arrange the crayfish tails on top. Place the noodles next to the crayfish, and a dressing of red caviar on top.

HILTON-RICHFIELD

Can you imagine a South African recipe only a few years ago calling for pink or green peppercorns? We have come a long way! Department of Useless Information: green peppercorns come either from Madagascar or Brazil, while the pink variety are exported mainly from the island of Réunion. (Black peppercorns would become white peppercorns if they were left to ripen.)

The Herbert Baker

Dysart House,
5 Winchester Road, Parktown 2193
Telephone: (011) 726-6253
PO Box 2395, Johannesburg 2000
Closed Saturday lunch
Fully licensed

Named after the English architect who created so many fine South African buildings early this century, the Herbert Baker nestles on the ground Floor of Dysart House in Parktown, Johannesburg; one of the great man's superb creations for private families.

It makes a lovely setting for a restaurant. The furnishings and décor are of the period, and the wood panelling is shown off to fine effect. Outside in the delightful gardens functions are held (when the weather's good) and inside, too, rooms are set aside for this purpose.

This is a restaurant planned and run by Alan and Hélène Gerson so that you can be assured not only of good food, but of access to one of the finest wine lists in South Africa. The ladies' bar is inviting and well-stocked, and when you eventually proceed to your beautifully-appointed table you are in the mood to enjoy some first-class cooking.

The menu is usually quite short, as it should be in this type of house, and is based squarely on the freshest and most seasonal of the produce available each day in the markets. In charge of the kitchen is a very clever young woman, Janel Telian, who can hold her own with the most expert chefs in the land.

Her touch is very noticeable: the cooking is done to meticulous standards of quality, while the presentations are less ostentatiously intricate than those one finds at most top professional kitchens. This gives the diner a feeling of relaxation, as if he were dining in an elegant private home – which of course he is, in a way!

The Herbert Baker is a rip-roaring success. The formula is good and the performance is appreciated by its crowds of happy clients.

Trout en Chemise

4 trout, deboned
½ hardboiled egg, chopped
parsley, chopped
4 large, thin crêpes
small piece gherkin, chopped
mayonnaise to bind
salt and pepper to taste
THE GARNISH:
watercress, mushrooms, butter,
lemon juice

METHOD:
1. Mix the egg, gherkin, parsley and seasoning, and bind with mayonnaise.
2. Stuff the trout with this mixture.
3. Tie some buttered greaseproof paper (the wrapping from a packet of butter is ideal) around each fish.
4. Bake in a hot oven, at 200°C, or poach in simmering water with flavouring vegetables just until tender (about 8 minutes).
5. Remove greaseproof paper and string, and roll each trout in a hot crêpe.
6. Lay fish on a hot dish, spoon lemon butter over them and serve with a garnish of watercress.
NB: A few chopped mushrooms lightly fried in butter make a good addition to the stuffing.

110

HILTON-RICHFIELD
One cold Sunday afternoon when you've nothing better to do, make a big bowl of pancake batter, and fry up a whole bunch of crêpes. Do as many as you can before your feet give in. Best to use a tiny crêpe pan, the right size for one person, but you should also have a supply of larger ones, as for this recipe. Separate them with a piece of the paper specially made for the job (such as they use in delicatessens to separate slices of meat), pile them in stacks and deep-freeze them. They'll keep for months.

Prawns with Ham and Celery

INGREDIENTS:

16 fair-sized prawns, deveined, but not
  shelled (unless preferred)
60 g onion, finely chopped
10 g celery, finely sliced
125 mℓ good veal stock
chopped parsley
60 mℓ olive oil
10 g green pepper, finely sliced
1 slice cooked ham, diced
50 mℓ dry white wine
bread for dipping in sauce

METHOD:

1. Heat the oil and fry the onion lightly:
do not allow to colour.
2. Add the sliced vegetables and the
diced ham. Pour in the wine. Reduce to
almost nothing.
3. Add the veal stock and cook until well-
flavoured. Put in the prawns. Poach until
tender.
4. Serve in soup plates with bread for
dipping.

HILTON-RICHFIELD

It's getting harder and harder to get hold of decent veal: even bones for stock. Although South Africans on the whole (despite the influence of considerable numbers of European-born immigrants) do not use much veal, a good veal stock is an absolute essential to fine home cooking. It's worthwhile searching around until you can find a butcher who will supply you (not the baby beef that's foisted off on us as veal).

Ask for bones with some of the less-flavoured flesh still on them. Have them cut up into smallish pieces. Put in a big pot, cover with cold water. A carrot, a couple of bayleaves, a big bouquet garni, a sprinkling of black peppercorns, and enough salt only to start the taste going, all go into the pot, too. Boil up, remove the scum a couple of times, then simmer for as long as you like. Finally, remove the bones and other detritus, reduce drastically over high heat, clarify the liquid by pouring it through a muslin, cool in a plastic bakkie, then deep-freeze. It should keep for months: certainly for several weeks.

111

Dunkeld West Shopping Centre
Jan Smuts Avenue,
Dunkeld, Johannesburg 2196
Telephone: (011) 442-8216
Closed Saturday lunch
Wine & Malt licence

Ile de France

What a pleasure to be able to report the wild success of this delightful restaurant!

French provincial cuisine, cooked and presented capably and professionally; an enormous menu, compared with the small cards available elsewhere; portions to satisfy the hungry without insulting the capacity; the pungent aromas of herbs emanating from the open-style kitchen area – you might think you were in a busy bistro in France itself.

The genius behind all this is the unique Marc Guébert, not only a Frenchman's Frenchman, but possibly the most expert operator in the business. Marc has had his ups and downs, his successes and his near-failures during his years in South Africa. Above all his culinary expertise, though, is a man of acute intelligence: he always learns from his errors. Marc Guébert knows to a degree what his customers will enjoy, and he provides it with élan, dash, and no doubt a good deal of satisfaction.

A lesser chef would be criticised for offering such a wide variety of dishes, but M. Guébert cannot be faulted. He has technical mastery over the kitchens and the storerooms and everything he serves is just-so. Here you will find the casserole dishes beloved of provincial France: daube of beef; cassoulet of lamb, duck and sausage; ragoût of rabbit; pigeon in red wine; and, of course, typical French treatments of fish and seafood.

Bouillabaisse here is the nearest thing to Marseille you will ever find. Bourride, occasionally, makes its appearance. Guébert's sole cooked with a red wine sauce (the recipe is overleaf) is gastronomically intriguing and works like a dream.

The trouble with the Ile de France is choosing your food. You go along all set in your mind as to what you're going to order, and you find Marc has some unexpected delight on the menu that tempts you away from your determined path. No matter – that's what dining out is all about.

113

Coquille St-Jacques au Pistil de Safran

INGREDIENTS:
24 large scallops with coral
8 large scallop shells
300 mℓ dry white wine
3 mℓ saffron threads
80 g grated Parmesan cheese
100 g butter
200 mℓ fish stocck (see "Standard Recipes")
2 chopped pickling-size onions
3 bunches baby spinach
400 mℓ cream, 100 mℓ of it whipped
50 g flour
50 g cold butter (extra, for sauce)

METHOD:
1. Thoroughly wash and clean the spinach. Blanch in boiling water for 2 minutes. Drain and refresh in cold water.
2. Cook the scallops in white wine, chopped onion, fish stock and saffron for about 8 to 10 minutes. Try to keep them slightly underdone and soft, as scallops tend to become rubbery when overcooked.
3. Warm up the spinach by tossing it in a pan of butter. Place some in each of the scallop shells. Add the scallops on top. Keep warm.

THE SAUCE:
4. Melt the butter in a saucepan, add the flour and cook gently for 10 minutes, stirring continuously.
5. Allow to cool down.
6. Add the stock you obtained from cooking the scallops. Stir well with a whisk over low heat. Bring to the boil and simmer gently for another 10 minutes.
7. Add the cream. Reduce by one-third. Check the seasoning. The sauce should now be reasonably thick and of a yellow colour.
8. Add the whipped cream to the sauce and pour over the scallops. Sprinkle the grated parmesan cheese over the sauce.
9. Place the shells full of scallops and sauce in a very hot oven, or under a salamander or grill, so as to glaze them ("gratiner") to a nice regular brown colour. Serve immediately.

> **HILTON-RICHFIELD**
> The difficulty about using real scallop shells you've collected over the years is that the sizes vary so wildly. Obviously you need eight all the same size. And they must be large, otherwise you wouldn't be able to get enough on to them. Of course, you can always use plastic shells, but if you're prepared to use plastic shells, what are you doing reading this book? Actually, we have seen real shells in packets at some of the supermarkets, all of identical size, though smallish.

114

Filet de Sole au Pinot Noir et aux Raisins

INGREDIENTS:
3 soles, 450 g – 500 g each
300 mℓ Pinot Noir wine
2 small pickling-size onions, chopped
200 g butter
a little oil
1 small bunch black grapes, peeled
500 mℓ cream
50 g roasted, flaked almonds
100 mℓ fish stock (see "Standard
   Recipes")
a little seasoned flour

METHOD:
1. Skin and fillet the soles (or get the fishmonger to do it). Keep the bones and skin, adding them to the fish stock which you will have warmed up before starting this recipe.
2. In a pan, place the chopped onions, the red wine and the fish stock. Bring to the boil, then reduce by half. Add the cream. Reduce until the sauce has thickened.
3. Roll the sole fillets in flour after seasoning them with salt and pepper, or shake them in seasoned flour in a plastic bag. Shake off excess flour. Fry them in a little butter and oil, keeping them slightly underdone and moist.
4. Place the sole fillets (3 per person) on individual plates. Cut the grapes in half and seed them. Arrange the grape halves on the fish fillets, lengthwise.
5. Keep warm in the oven for a few minutes.
6. Just before serving, coat the fish with the sauce, first checking on the seasoning. Sprinkle the roasted almond slivers on top of the sauce. Decorate with a sprig of parsley and a flower made from a radish.

HILTON-RICHFIELD

Marc Guébert was the first professional chef in South Africa, as far as we know, to use red wine in a fish recipe — and with a delicately flavoured sole, what's more! This cuts right across the popular fallacy that only white wine goes with fish.

There are some excellent pinot noir wines on the market now. This is the grape from which all the wines of Burgundy are made. On a hot summer's day, try drinking one slightly chilled, instead of the old belief that red wine has to be at (South African!) room temperature.

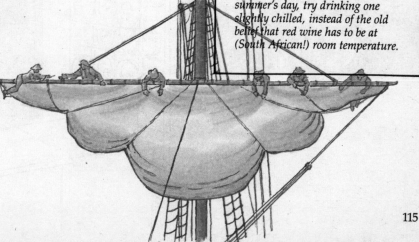

115

Tropicana Hotel ★★★★ TYYY
85 Marine Parade, Durban 4001
Telephone: (031) 37-6261
Closed Sundays
Fully licensed

La Concha

*D*urban, of course, is the holiday-maker's mecca. There are hotels at every level of the scale, to cater for the varying amount of spending-money each visitor bring with him. There are the five-star caravanserais, there are the cheap-and-nasty doss-houses (with no view of the sea), and there are several good hotels bang in the middle of the spectrum.

Somehow, one doesn't expect to find really tip-top food in any but the most expensive rooms. That's illogical, of course, and no restaurant will prove it more conclusively than La Concha.

The Tropicana is purely a holiday hotel, situated right on the waterfront of South Beach, and La Concha can hardly be described as an elegant restaurant. Atmosphere-wise, it's rather on the plain side. Little attempt has been made to create anything other than a simple ambience – wisely, for this is a tiny room. But what surprisingly excellent seafood you find here!

Robert Knowles is a young English chef who has created this varied and delightful menu of fish and shellfish dishes. The cynical might say that it's easy to create a menu, but what about the cooking? They need have no fears when Mr Knowles is at his stoves. The realisation of his creations is excellent. His use of spices and seasonings displays the sure hand of the natural cook: he's not frightened to give the food a taste!

In his enthusiasm, Robert gave us several fish recipes to choose from for this book, and we found it hard to select two that we thought you, the reader, might enjoy more than the others.

Try La Concha when next you visit Durban's sea-front. It's a very good room indeed.

Platter "Bimini"

INGREDIENTS:
200 g fillet of beef, finely sliced
200 g chicken breast, finely sliced
200 g prawns, out of the shell,
   deveined
1 medium green pepper, in strips
250 mℓ long-grain rice, cooked your
   own way, and kept in the fridge until
   needed
30 mℓ soy sauce (use the cheaper,
   cooking type)
100 g bamboo shoot, drained, cut into
   pieces
1 small onion, finely diced
150 g butter
50 mℓ white wine
watercress for garnish
salt and pepper to taste

METHOD:
1. Melt 100 g butter in a pan, add most of the onion (reserve a little) and the white wine and reduce by half. Add the green pepper.
2. Season the fillet steak, chicken and prawns with salt and pepper.
3. First, add the fillet steak to the mixture, and cook quickly to seal.
4. Now add the chicken breasts and cook for 2 minutes.
5. Now add the prawns and cook for a further 2 minutes.
6. Add soy sauce, just enough to brown the mixture. Add the bamboo shoot and let mixture simmer for 2 minutes, stirring continuously.
7. Put the rest of the butter (50 g) in another pan with the rest of the chopped onion. Stir-fry the cooked rice in this mixture. Check that the rice does not stick, even if you are using a teflon-based pan.
8. Put the rice on a serving platter and place mixture on top. Garnish with watercress.

HILTON-RICHFIELD
An interesting, piquant recipe. If you would like to add a touch of typical Chinese sweetness to the sauce, you can add two or three little metal utensils* of Hoisin Sauce at Step 6. You can buy it at any Chinese grocery.

   *Sorry, we are not allowed by law to say "teaspoonfuls".

Croûte "Rothschild"

INGREDIENTS:

1 loaf of stale white bread, crusts removed
1 x 500 g crayfish
4 large king prawns, out of shell, deveined (about 200 g)
4 button mushrooms, sliced
100 mℓ lobster bisque (canned or fresh) or crayfish sauce (see "Standard Recipes") with extra cream
4 knobs of butter
bunch watercress (or parsley)
½ small onion, chopped
25 mℓ cognac or brandy
80 mℓ Hollandaise sauce (see "Standard Recipes")
dash of Pernod
2 lemons
oil for frying

METHOD:

1. Slice the loaf into four equal blocks and hollow out each block carefully, using a small sharp knife. Make the walls and base as thin as you can manage.
2. Deep-fry the bread baskets in hot oil at 190°C until golden brown inside and out.
3. Drain on a paper towel and keep in the warming drawer.
4. Melt the knobs of butter in a pan and gently sweat the onion in the melted butter for 2 minutes.
5. Cut the crayfish tail into 8 pieces, and add.
6. Cut the prawns in halves and add. Put the lid on the pan and sweat for 2 minutes.
7. Add the brandy and a dash of Pernod. (Heat it first!) Flame, then reduce the sauce by one-half.
8. Add the mushrooms. Pour the bisque into the pan and simmer for 3 minutes.
9. Spoon into each basket of fried bread in equal portions. Mask the top of each basket with a layer of Hollandaise sauce and brown under a hot overhead grill.
10. Garnish each "croûton" with a sprig of watercress or parsley, half a lemon star, and serve immediately on a hot fish plate.

HILTON-RICHFIELD

Lobster bisque — you can buy it in tins, but if you've saved up all the crayfish, prawn and shrimp shells and bits and pieces, and kept them in your deep-freezer, perhaps now's the time to take them all out, boil them up, add them to any crayfish sauce you've already made, stir in some cream, and there you are! If you can afford — and find — a container of Lobster Base made by L H Minor, of Cleveland, Ohio, so much the better. There's nothing in the world as good or as quick and handy.

119

3 Rivonia Road, Illovo 2196
Telephone: (011) 788-5264
PO Box 55452, Northlands 2116
Closed Saturday lunch and Sundays
Fully licenced

La Margaux

A long-established restaurant in the heart of the affluent Illovo area of northern Johannesburg. Its name should, of course, be "Le Margaux": the mistake was made by the original owners, and over the years no-one has thought it necessary to correct it.

This grammatical carelessness most definitely does not carry through to the excellent kitchen, the meticulously correct service, and the superb quality of the fresh produce proudly and tastefully displayed on a centre table.

With an Italian owner who is a long-time pro at the game, and a French name, the menu (as might be expected) is a bow in both directions. You will not find better pasta and other Italian specialities; nor will you find better presentations of classical French dishes, or more appetisingly fresh linefish.

The tables are comfortably spaced around a large room on the first floor of a small centre: there is plenty of parking. The room's appointments fall short of ostentatious luxury but are exactly what an upper-crust restaurant of this quality should have. Comfort is the watchword here, both in the furnishings and the ambience.

The wine-list is extensive, offering many famous French marques at prices that are lower than at most places. This is deliberate: here, wine is something to go with a good meal, and not meant merely as an opporunity for the vulgar to show off.

Altogether a most superior restaurant, with a clientèle consisting largely of people who have been made to feel comfortable here over many years.

Kabeljou Mistral

INGREDIENTS:
800 g fresh kabeljou fillets
150 g mushrooms, thinly sliced
100 mℓ dry white wine
40 g breadcrumbs
200 g tomatoes, skinned, deseeded and
    chopped
1 clove garlic, crushed
200 mℓ olive oil
salt and pepper, flour for coating

METHOD:
1. Cut up the kabeljou into slices 25 mm thick.
2. Place the flour, salt and pepper in a plastic bag. Drop the slices of kob in, and shake. Remove the fish and shake off excess flour.
3. Heat about 100 mℓ of the olive oil in a flat pan. Quickly fry the slices of fish so as to seal them, but not to cook them.
4. In a separate pan, heat the remaining oil. Sauté the mushrooms, add the garlic, then the tomatoes. Soften them.
5. Arrange the slices of fish in a flat, ovenproof dish and add the tomato, garlic and mushroom mixture. Moisten with white wine and sprinkle with the breadcrumbs. Sprinkle with the remaining oil, and finish off the cooking by browning under the grill.

> **HILTON-RICHFIELD**
> *This is a classic recipe from the Côte d'Azur, where they usually use large red mullet. Some chefs in the South of France add grated Gruyère cheese to the breadcrumbs, which adds another dimension to the glazing under the grill.*

Linefish Paprika

(kabeljou, yellowtail, geelbek, stompnose, steenbras, etc)

INGREDIENTS:
4 nice-sized fillets of fish
5 mℓ paprika
100 mℓ oil
15 mℓ flour
3 mℓ salt
1 English cucumber thinly sliced

THE SAUCE:
45 mℓ oil
2 tomatoes, skinned, deseeded,
   chopped
10 mℓ paprika
10 mℓ tomato purée
125 mℓ sour cream
5 onions, chopped finely
2 cloves garlic, crushed
30 mℓ flour
200 mℓ white wine
salt and pepper to taste

METHOD:
1. Dry the fillets of fish. Shake them in a plastic bag in which you have put the mixture of flour, salt and paprika. Shake off excess.
2. Heat the oil. Place the fish in the pan and brown it all over. Reduce the heat drastically and cook the fish for about 10 minutes, gently.

THE SAUCE:
3. Heat the oil in a flameproof pan with a lid. Add onions to the pan and cook gently. Do not allow them to colour.
4. Add garlic and tomatoes. Sprinkle with flour and paprika, season with salt and pepper, and stir in the tomato purée. Add wine, cook through, then add cream. Cover, and cook gently for 20 minutes.

SERVICE:
Arrange the fish on a serving dish. Stir the sour cream into the pan. Heat it without allowing it to boil. Pour the sauce over the fish, and surround the dish with a continuous line of very thinly sliced cucumber.

> **HILTON-RICHFIELD**
> *All praise to whomever it was, a few years ago, who first started growing those long, thin, English cucumbers in South Africa. The price can be fierce sometimes, but they taste so much better than the coarse, short, stumpy cucumbers we had been used to. And how spectacular those thin, regular slices are, when you've put a whole English cucumber through your food processor. In the old days of hand-slicing, it took an age to get through a cucumber. Now it only takes a few seconds — but an age to arrange the slices accurately around the dish! The effect is well worth the trouble, though.*

15 Gillespie Street,
Durban 4001
Telephone: (031) 32-7887
Closed Saturday lunch and Sundays
Fully licensed

La Popote

Victor Janssen is one of the senior restaurateurs of Durban. In the days when there was hardly a decent privately-owned à la carte room to be found in that city, Victor led the way with this fine little restaurant down in Gillespie Street. Its provender was enjoyed over a long period by a large coterie of regular customers.

There have been changes, but nothing earth-shaking as far as the satisfaction of the diner is concerned. In the first place, La Popote moved a couple of doors down the road to its present premises. In the second place, Mr Janssen wisely seized the opportunity offered to him when the new restaurant at the revamped Playhouse became available. (*See L'Artiste.*)

Victor is still the owner, but the real chef-patron is his chef of some years now, Graeme Mitchell, who with his wife runs La Popote most efficiently.

Trained in Britain, one of the new wave of dedicated young chefs which that country has been turning out over the past decade-and-a-half, Graeme is a disciple of the traditional French school.

His cooking can't be faulted. If the clientèle of La Popote were more adventurous, and were prepared to pay for it, he could most certainly turn out great dishes closer to the concept of "haute cuisine", but the restaurant is quite content (as it should be) to continue providing Durbanites and visitors with a very high class of French provincial cooking in this pleasant room.

A thoroughly satisfactory dining experience can always be had at La Popote.

125

Black Mushrooms with Tuna and Tomato

INGREDIENTS:
8 large black mushrooms
2 x 210 g cans tuna
1 x 425 g can tomato purée, or 4 large
   tomatoes, blanched, skinned,
   deseeded and chopped
3 mℓ chopped parsley
2 cloves garlic, crushed
3 mℓ basil, chopped
100 g Gruyère cheese, grated
100 g butter
salt and freshly ground black pepper
   to taste

METHOD:
1. Soften the butter and combine with the crushed garlic.
2. Wash the mushrooms thoroughly, remove their stalks, melt the garlic butter in a pan, and fry the mushrooms. Allow to cool.
3. Add the tuna fish to the chopped tomato and put in the blender.
4. Add the basil, chopped parsley, salt and pepper.
5. When all ingredients are well-blended, remove the mixture and spread it on the tops of the mushrooms. Cover with Gruyère cheese and grill.

HILTON-RICHFIELD

Strange how fashions in food change. A few years ago, everyone thought that only tiny, white button mushrooms were the things to use. Gourmets have always known, though, that the brown, coarser mushrooms are tastier and much stronger in flavour. Now, the pendulum has swung so widely that many restaurants offer as a starter big, black mushrooms, be-garlicked, be-herbed and be-flavoured so strongly that they often spoil the palate for the dishes to follow. This recipe is a pleasant compromise between blandness and piquancy, however. And the addition of tuna is very fashionable! It's the fastest-selling canned fish of its type.

Kingklip "Cecilia"

INGREDIENTS:
4 kingklip fillets, about 250 g each
4 egg yolks (keep the whites: see note)
250 g butter
a little flour
salt and pepper to taste
1 can large asparagus spears, drained
30 mℓ white wine
100 g Parmesan cheese
sauce Hollandaise (see "Standard
  Recipes")

METHOD:
1. Combine the salt and pepper with the flour in a plastic bag. Shake the kingklip fillets in it. Remove, and shake off excess flour.
2. Melt the butter in a large pan and fry the fish until cooked. Be careful when turning them over as kingklip is inclined to stick.
3. Take 4 large asparagus spears and cut them carefully in halves, down the stalks. Place 2 half-spears on each piece of fish, diagonally. Cover with sauce Hollandaise, sprinkle with Parmesan cheese and brown lightly under a hot grill.

HILTON-RICHFIELD
If you should be reading this during the fresh asparagus season, put all thought of using canned asparagus out of your mind. Our South African "grass" is the equal of any in the world, and whether you use the white spears (which have not been allowed to shoot up into the sunlight) or the green spears (which have had a few hours in the air), you'll find them infinitely more acceptable than tinned "grass". If you do use fresh spears, though, remember to scrape the stalks properly and cut them off well above the base, so that every bit may be eaten. (Keep the scrapings and the stalk-bottoms for soup.) Cook them until not quite soft enough to eat and keep until needed for this recipe. The final process of glazing under the grill will complete the cooking.
  Note: The best way to keep your unused egg-whites is in a well-dried bottle, tightly sealed. Kept in the fridge, they'll last up to 1 month. They can also be frozen and kept for ages. The white of an extra-large egg is about 40 mℓ.

The Playhouse,
Smith Street, Durban 4001
Telephone: (031) 304-3296
PO Box 385, Durban 4000
Closed Saturday lunch and Sundays
Fully licensed

l'Artiste

What an exercise in nostalgia is this lovely restaurant! Up on the first floor and the gallery of the revamped Playhouse in Smith Street, you walk into another world. What seems like acres of oak panelling cover the extensive walls. The furnishings are heavy and bring the 1930s back into view. The artefacts on display, the pictures and programmes, actually recall that era.

And if you are as old as we are, and you ever lived in Cape Town when the Del Monico restaurant was there opposite the Alhambra Theatre, run by Mr Bagatta, l'Artiste will tumble you straight into bitter-sweet memories of what has gone, what can never be recalled. It is the Del Monico personified. It is a living monument to the 1930s.

If that were all, the place would be an interesting relic and nothing more. The authorities, however, saw fit to place the running of l'Artiste in the hands of Victor Janssen (*see La Popote*), a doyen of Durban restaurateurs, a highly experienced professional whose touch is sure and delicate.

So far, the public has taken to l'Artiste as if it had always been there. The food is splendid, the service equally good (it is difficult to find bad service in Durban, with its wealth of Indian waiters) and the menu as imaginative as a restaurant of this calibre needs. It should continue to do well. The entire Playhouse operation is a marvel of planning and good taste, and the same qualities have gone into the complex's catering facilities. Congratulations to the Durban authorities. They are certainly leading the way.

Terrine de l'Opéra

INGREDIENTS:
SCALLOP MIXTURE:
200 g scallops, finely minced
100 mℓ double cream
1 medium egg
50 mℓ mild fish stock (see "Standard Recipes")
FISH MIXTURE:
300 g kingklip or other white fish, finely minced
2 medium eggs
fresh dill, finely chopped
5 mℓ Dijon mustard
150 mℓ double cream
100 mℓ fish stock (see "Standard Recipes")
10 mℓ green peppercorns

METHOD:
Make both mixtures separately, but in the same way.
1. Beat the minced fish until smooth, then mix in the cream, eggs, and fish stock. Season to taste.
2. Line the base of a large terrine with greaseproof paper. Grease the paper. Spoon in the scallop mixture first, cover with the kingklip mixture. Seal with a large sheet of greased foil, and chill for one hour (this is necessary to let it rest and "come together").
3. Preheat the oven to 170°C. Place the terrine in a large baking pan of water (bain-marie). Bake for about 30 to 40 minutes until firm.
4. Allow to cool to room temperature; later, in the fridge.

HILTON-RICHFIELD
Remember that when making a terrine, pâté or mousse, all the ingredients must be very cold, and you must work quickly: otherwise it all goes gunge-like. The word "terrine", incidentally, is really the earthenware container you make the pâté in (from the French word "terre", meaning "earth"). By usage, though, these days it has come to mean the pâté itself. (Another astonishing fact from the Department of Useless Information.)

Crêpes "Macbeth"

INGREDIENTS:
CREPE MIXTURE:
100 g flour
125 mℓ water
2 egg yolks, in addition
10 mℓ each chopped parsley, chives and
    dill
8 slices smoked salmon
125 mℓ milk
5 eggs
50 g melted butter
5 mℓ salt
SPRING ONION SAUCE:
1 bunch spring onions, washed and
    chopped
15 mℓ white wine
2 tomatoes, blanched, skinned,
    seeded, chopped
20 g butter
10 g extra butter, chilled
250 mℓ cream
1 onion, chopped
salt and white pepper to taste

METHOD:
1. Mix all crêpe ingredients together, and beat until very smooth. Keep cool for at least an hour before using. Fry crêpes in usual way, but on a lower heat than normal, so as to prevent the herbs from burning.
2. Fry onion in a little butter. Add the white wine. Reduce sauce by half. Add cream. Reduce by half again. Season, and add chopped tomato and chopped spring onions.
3. Add the extra butter to thicken the sauce slightly. Do not allow to boil again.
4. Place the crêpes on serving plates, open. Arrange the smoked salmon slices on one half of each crêpe. Fold over. Spoon sauce on to unoccupied half of plate. Garnish with spring onion stems.

HILTON-RICHFIELD
Strange how few good recipes there are using spring onions. The northern Chinese use them a great deal (in Peking — now known as "Beijin" — cooking). They add a definite piquancy to this pleasant pancake recipe. And remember there is a wide world of taste and texture between really good smoked salmon and the usually fairly low-quality, locally smoked varieties. Don't blame the recipe if your salmon isn't the best.

The Mall, Rosebank
Johannesburg 2196
Telephone: (011) 788-8400
Closed Saturday lunch and Sundays
Wine and Malt licence

Le Francais

*T*his delightful room was the first restaurant in South Africa to present French provincial cooking to South African audiences. Not the spurious, pseudo-French, half-hearted cookery that many others offered, but the full-flavoured, uncompromisingly Gallic food that you find in France itself.

Over the years the standard has never dropped, and Le Français continues to be a leader in the field. The new owners, who took over in mid-1986, are Ian and Mary McDowell, a young English couple. Their story is a very heart-warming one.

The McDowells were brought to South Africa a few years ago from London by Le Français, he to work as assistant chef, she to share front-of-house duties with the owners. Ian had been trained by the great Rémy Fougère, the famous French teaching chef who has run the 5-star Royal Garden Hotel in Kensington for over 12 years now. His experience has all been in 5-star kitchens, but he adapted himself excellently to the rather different conditions of the kitchen in a small, privately-owned restaurant. He did very well.

So that when the ex-owners decided to proceed to other fields, it was logical to offer the restaurant to the McDowells. What a pleasant story! From sous-chef to chef-patron in a couple of swiftly-passing years!

The standard of McDowell's cooking is most impressive. He has been steeped in the traditions of the food of the French provinces, and he translates them with skill and instinctive good taste to the South African ambience. His pretty wife Mary has a sweet personality and a shy charm that has endeared her to the diners here.

Neither of these delightful Londoners are exuberant, flamboyant restaurateurs in the Mediterranean mould, but dedicated professionals quietly going about their task of providing Johannesburg with some of its finest French food.

133

Crayfish in a Shrimp and Pernod Sauce

INGREDIENTS:
8 small crayfish (or 4 large)
300 g uncooked shrimps, deveined
200 m*l* Pernod
100 g butter, cut into chunks
50 g butter (for spinach)
50 g fresh tarragon (or 20 g dried)
1 bunch spinach
250 m*l* strong fish stock (see "Standard Recipes")
250 m*l* cream
3 m*l* saffron threads soaked in a little hot water
2 *l* court-bouillon (see "Standard Recipes")

METHOD:
1. Cook crayfish in the court-bouillon until dark red.
2. Break tail away from head. Keep warm. (Reserve head for stock).
3. Sauté shrimps in a little butter. Pour on the Pernod and flame. Keep warm.
4. Remove shell from crayfish and slice thickly, angling knife at about 45°. Keep warm, covered.
5. Thoroughly clean the spinach, remove thicker stalks, and sauté in 50 g butter. (It will be quicker with the lid on.)

134

(Save a little spinach for the garnish.)
6. Place spinach in serving dish, spread out, and place the crayfish slices on top. Place shrimps on top of crayfish.
7. To the Pernod and butter in which the shrimps were sautéed, add the fish stock. Boil and reduce by half.
8. Place crayfish in oven to heat through.
9. Add cream to sauce and reduce by half again.
10. Finish sauce with the cold butter (add it while sauce is still boiling).
11. Add chopped tarragon. Coat crayfish with sauce and serve.

THE GARNISH:
Heat the frying pan, add small amount of butter. Take left-over spinach and shred it finely. Add to pan, season and toss quickly. Do not cook until soggy and colour is lost.

HILTON-RICHFIELD
Ian McDowell, English born and trained, is a most accomplished young chef, who now owns the famous Johannesburg restaurant Le Français, after coming out from the UK, as assistant chef, only a couple of years ago! He is a swift, efficient and imaginative chap, who prefers the steamy atmosphere of the kitchen to making small talk with the customers. Happily, his pretty wife, Mary, runs the dining-room, and she is charm itself.

Monkfish with Chive Sauce

INGREDIENTS:
500 g – 600 g monkfish (4 medium
  sized fish)
70 g onion, chopped
15 g butter
250 mℓ white wine
250 mℓ fish stock (see "Standard
  Recipes")
1 bunch chives, chopped
70 g cold butter, for finishing
4 leeks, cut into thin rings (white only)

METHOD:
1. If the skin is not removed from fish,
ask your fishmonger to do it, as it is a
messy job on the monkfish. Remove the
fish from the bone, so that you have two
fillets from each fish (or, again, get the
fishmonger to do it for you). Cut each
fillet into pieces about 50 mm long.
2. Grease an oven-pan with butter and
lay fish in it. Cover with chopped onion
and leek rings. Season. Add white wine
and fish stock. Cover with buttered
paper. Poach gently at 180°C in the oven
for 10 to 15 minutes.
3. When cooked, remove the fish (it
should be soft). Pour sauce into saucepan and reduce by half.

4. Add remaining butter (very cold)
whisking all the time. Add finely
chopped chives. Coat fish and serve.

HILTON-RICHFIELD
*Monkfish isn't available as often as
one would like. It's a firm, white fish
with an extraordinary amount of
liquid in the flesh. It needs a lot of
seasoning. You can easily cut it into
scallops, egg-and-breadcrumb it, and
fry it. If you should ever catch one,
you might be tempted to throw it
back, because it's an ugly brute with
a big mouth and lots of teeth. Its
other name is "anglerfish", because of
its nasty manner towards smaller
fish and the way it catches them.*

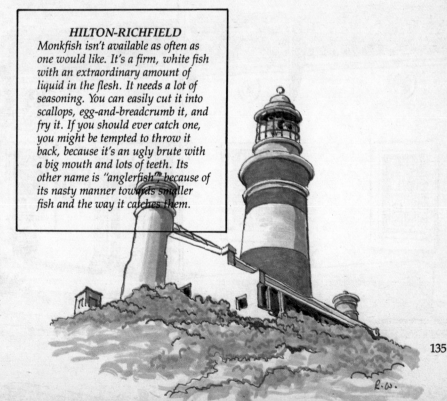

R. Wab '86

16 Huguenot Road,
Franschhoek 7690
Telephone: (02212) 2248
PO Box 237, Franschhoek 7690
Closed Mondays, Tuesdays and Sunday evenings

Le Quartier Francais

*I*t's hard to think of a restaurant that has achieved a greater reputation, and gathered more accolades, than this pretty room in the village of Franschhoek.

The beautiful valley itself has sprung to the fore recently with its good wines, and particularly because among the owners of the wine estates here are some very experienced advertising and marketing people! Le Quartier Francais, though, can stand triumphantly on its own two feet, for it is one of the most superior restaurants in the Cape.

Adré McWilliam Smith and her husband Arthur are the owners, and, respectively, chef and maître. The redoubtable Adré is responsible for several unique features. She is, first of all, cordon bleu-trained and has not been through the rigours of a professional hotel school: that in itself is uncommon enough.

Then this clever lady has woven together a small menu that combines the delicacy of modern French cuisine with the more robust cookery of the Cape. This seemingly incongruous juxtaposition works splendidly in the hands of a cook whose palate, obviously, appreciates the subtleties of seasoning and spicing so completely.

The menu-card does nothing to prepare you for the feast to come. There are only a few items (this in itself breeds confidence in a small restaurant) and their descriptions are so simple that they sound almost banal. But this is the art that conceals art, and the food that's presented on the plate satisfies the eye, the tastebuds and the soul!

Though you'll eat heartily and satisfyingly, do leave space for a sweet. At Le Quartier, there are some beauties and they should be sampled.

Altogether a lovely little restaurant that deserves its big reputation.

137

Red Steenbras in White Wine Sauce

(Kabeljou or stumpnose may be used instead)

INGREDIENTS:

600 – 700 g red steenbras, skinned, filleted
1 kg fresh spinach
200 mℓ dry white wine
a little butter (to re-heat spinach)
4 ripe tomatoes
300 mℓ fish stock (see "Standard Recipes")
200 mℓ cream
5 fresh basil leaves (or 3 mℓ dried basil)
pinch of sugar
salt and pepper

METHOD:

1. Peel and slice tomatoes, squeeze out all pips.
2. Melt a little butter and cook tomato with a little salt, pepper, a pinch of sugar and basil until the tomatoes are soft. Set aside.
3. Cut out stems of spinach. Wash well in running water. Place in salted boiling water and cook for 5 minutes. Drain and refresh spinach under running cold water.
4. Squeeze out moisture in a cloth or between your hands. (The above may be done well in advance.)
5. Cut fish into serving pieces. Salt and pepper lightly.
6. Place in pan with approximately 300 mℓ fish stock and 200 mℓ dry white wine. Cover with buttered greaseproof paper. Poach fish gently for about 10 minutes or until the fish is done.
7. Lift the fish out of the poaching liquid and keep warm.
8. Turn up heat and reduce liquid so that it becomes more concentrated.
9. Add 200 mℓ cream and reduce again until the consistency is like that of thin cream.
10. Taste for salt and pepper. Strain if not smooth.
11. Reheat spinach in a little melted butter. Also reheat tomatoes.
12. Place a piece of steenbras on each warmed plate. Coat with the white wine sauce so that it covers the base of the plate.
13. Place about a serving-spoonful of buttered spinach on top of each piece of fish. Finish by placing a spoonful of the tomatoes on top of the spinach. Serve at once.

HILTON-RICHFIELD
This meticulous recipe is as close to "haute cuisine française" as you're likely to reach in this country. It's typical of the careful and painstaking cooking that Le Quartier Français has become famous for. All it needs is some of those nice little sauce-spoons you see in France these days — about the size of a large dessertspoon, with the left-hand edge cut away to a straight line, so that you can slurp up the sauce from the plate without indulging in that disgusting, vulgar, peasant habit of wiping the plate clean with a piece of bread. (We confess, though, that bread-wiping brings much more fundamental satisfaction.)

Smoked Snoek Crêpes

INGREDIENTS:
2 egg yolks
10 mℓ brandy
65 mℓ milk
500 mℓ béchamel sauce (see "Standard Recipes")
250 g grated Swiss Gruyère cheese (for sprinkling on top of the crêpes)
15 mℓ melted butter
70 g flour
75 mℓ water
pinch salt

METHOD:
1. Put the milk, egg yolks and water in a processor and mix together.
2. Add the flour, brandy, salt and melted butter and mix well.
3. Put aside in fridge for an hour or two (or overnight).
4. Fry very thin pancakes.

THE SNOEK FILLING:
20 mℓ chopped shallots or spring onions
250 g flaked smoked snoek
35 mℓ flour
45 mℓ butter
100 mℓ dry white wine
5 mℓ chopped tarragon
250 mℓ boiling milk
salt and pepper to taste

METHOD:
1. Melt butter and sauté spring onions over low heat for a few minutes.
2. Add white wine and reduce to a syrup. Add flour, stirring in with a wire whisk.
3. Add boiling milk and stir well. Bring to the boil.
4. Fold in flaked smoked snoek and tarragon. Taste for seasoning.

TO ASSEMBLE:
1. Place approximately 30 mℓ of the smoked snoek filling on each crêpe and then roll it up.
2. Place the rolled crêpes in a buttered oven dish. Cover with béchamel sauce and sprinkle with grated Gruyère cheese.
3. Place in a preheated oven at 180°C for 20 minutes, or until crêpes are heated through and cheese is melted.

HILTON-RICHFIELD
Watch the salt in the crêpe mixture: the amount will depend on the quality of the smoked snoek you use. Some of it on the market is dreadful; so salty that you need a mouthwash afterwards. Stick to a make you can trust, like the excellent Cape Coast Brand. If the snoek is very salty, don't use any salt at all in the crêpe mixture.

12 Fredman Drive,
Sandown 2196
Telephone: (011) 783-8947
PO Box 785962, Sandton 2146
Closed Saturday lunch and Sundays
Fully licensed

Les Marquis

One of the most beautiful and elegant dining-rooms in the country, Les Marquis is that rare creature: a restaurant designed as a restaurant and built by professional restaurant people.

Germain Marquis is as French as the Eiffel Tower, as Gallic as boeuf bourguignonne. His accent is pronounced, his gestures unmistakeably Parisian, and almost his entire staff reflect his Frenchness. Not all, for this magnificent room is under the benign control of Bill Berry, a maître d'hôtel of great style and skill whose Anglo-Saxon characteristics contrast strongly with the Gallic atmosphere here.

The food is French, French, French right the way through. It is cooked and presented by a brigade of young French chefs who were brought out here by Germain Marquis for the purpose. Their wives work here, too: as waitresses, in the wine bar, at the front door. The overall effect is highly competent, professional cooking, presented with flair and finesse, and served with all the skill that top European training engenders.

But this is not a room for pot-cooking, for little "marmites" of casseroles and stews. This is not a bistro; this is an up-market home of "haute cuisine", and you must expect the prices to reflect that level of gastronomy. They are not high prices, though, and by comparison with the rest of the world, surprisingly low.

You can easily double the cost of your meal by choosing a couple of bottles of Germain's famous-label French wines, but why should you? There are low-priced French marques available and a plethora of labels from the Cape, and there is also highly-skilled advice to help you select a wine that's suitable.

This lovely restaurant could be picked up and set down in the heart of Paris and do well there. It is truly a little bit of French flair in the heart of Sandton.

Cape Salmon "Huguenot"

INGREDIENTS:
4 x 200 g Cape salmon, filleted
1 small onion, finely diced
5 mℓ fresh thyme
250 g butter
30 mℓ fish fumet (see "Standard
  Recipes")
500 g young spinach
120 g slices of bone marrow, 5 mm
  thick
300 mℓ good red wine
50 mℓ oil
250 mℓ fresh tomato, peeled, pipped
  and liquidised
Mushrooms for duxelles (about 200 g)
  (see note)
pinch sugar
salt and pepper to taste

METHOD:
1. Dry the fish fillets, add salt and pepper, dredge with flour, shake off excess.
2. Warm a little oil in a frying pan together with 50 g of the butter. When it begins to foam, put the fish fillets in, skin-side first, and pan-fry gently on both sides for 2 minutes a side.
3. Sprinkle with thyme. Put in preheated oven at 180°C for about 12 minutes.
4. During this operation, put your slices of bone-marrow in a pan, cover with salted water, and heat. Remove when it starts to boil and cool under running water.

THE SAUCE:
5. Sweat the diced onion in 30 mℓ oil and 15 g of the remaining butter. Deglaze (see note) the pan with red wine. Add fish stock and tomato. Let reduce slowly. Strain to remove the onion, and add a pinch of sugar if too acid. Season with salt and pepper, with emphasis on the pepper.
6. Add the remaining butter bit by bit and whisk it into the mixture.

TO SERVE:
Pour the sauce over the fillets and put the slice of marrow on top.

142

Fillet of Red Roman à la Niçoise

(A light summer starter)

INGREDIENTS:
2 x 500 g red roman, filleted
2 cloves garlic, crushed
1 medium onion, thinly sliced
60 mℓ red wine vinegar
pinch cayenne pepper
250 mℓ olive oil
15 mℓ coriander seeds
2 medium carrots, very thinly sliced
125 mℓ water
3 mℓ fresh thyme, chopped
garlic toast
salt, freshly ground black pepper, to
    taste

METHOD:
1. Remove all bones from fish with a pair of tweezers. Cut fillets in halves, lengthwise. Dry them well.
2. Pour the olive oil into a pan and bring to medium heat. Fry the red roman fillets, turning carefully until slightly golden in colour. Remove, and place in suitable terrine or glass dish.
3. Place the onion, carrots and garlic in the oil and fry gently. Remove pan from stove, add vinegar, water, thyme, cayenne pepper, coriander seeds, salt and pepper. Replace on stove and boil for a few minutes.
4. Pour over the fish. Let mixture cool down, then place in refrigerator.
NOTE: This dish keeps very well if the fish is well-covered by the oil, and the dish is sealed with plastic-wrap. Can be kept for up to 10 days.

TO SERVE:
Present the dish with some fresh toasted bread perfumed slightly with garlic, a nice salad of butter lettuce, green beans, tomatoes and olives, and some anchovies on the side.

HILTON-RICHFIELD
Although Germain Marquis puts the anchovies stone last, as a sort of afterthought, the dish can't be called "niçoise" without them. Anchovies aren't used as often as they might be, it seems to us. Their best use is like this, as a starter or hors d'oeuvre, because otherwise their saltiness might upset the palate's balance. Make them go further, though, by cutting them carefully down the centre with a very, very sharp knife.

Maharani Hotel ★★★★★ TYYY
83 Snell Parade, Durban 4001
Telephone: (031) 32-7361
PO Box 10592, Marine Parade 4056
Closed Sundays and all lunchtimes
Fully licensed

Les Saisons

Durban's newest, smartest, most up-market restaurant which, by some considerable cunning, still manages to be informal and warmly welcoming.

The décor is in pastel shades of green: a shade which is carried through even to the carpeting. The effect is something like a conservatory, albeit without plants, and it's very restful. The central well presents a display of fresh produce: fresh fish every day, superb cuts of the finest meats, and all the salad and garnish items you would expect at a five-star restaurant.

There are alcoves at the side of the gracious room, and you may sit in them watching the passing parade, or use the space as a secluded, private dining-room.

Although Les Saisons presents a menu of international and classical restaurant favourites, its philosophy follows the seasons, and stress is always on the fruits of the sea,

the land and the skies that are abundant at appropriate times of the year. This is the European pattern for first-class rooms and it is good to see it followed here.

Patrons of Les Saisons are top business-people and, of course, holiday-makers, too. So, in addition to its à la carte list, the restaurant also offers a table d'hôte menu, with a choice of three soups, three hors d'oeuvre, three main courses and a tempting array of desserts. Members of the WHB (Well-Heeled Brigade) are just as price-conscious these days as we ordinary folk, and the set meals at Les Saisons are proving a great attraction.

Oysters, crayfish, mussels, clams, langoustines and prawns all feature prominently, of course, and Durban suppliers are vying with each other to get a foot in this upper-market venue. Les Saisons will be with us for many seasons to come.

Red Roman Soup

INGREDIENTS:

4 fillets of red roman, medium sized
15 mℓ flour
1 clove garlic, minced or crushed
15 mℓ fresh parsley, finely chopped
3 mℓ dried basil
250 mℓ dry white wine
30 g butter
1 large onion, coarsely chopped
1 bayleaf
3 mℓ thyme, dried
750 mℓ water
6 large tomatoes, peeled and coarsely
  chopped
salt and freshly ground black pepper

METHOD:

1. Melt butter in a large heavy pot. Add chopped onion and cook until just tender.
2. Blend in flour and stir constantly until browned, over low heat.
3. Add tomatoes and all seasoning to pot, plus salt and pepper to taste.
4. Cook for a few minutes until tomatoes are soft.
5. Add water and bring mixture to just below boiling point.
6. Sprinkle red roman fillets with salt and pepper. Add the fish to the tomato mixture, reduce heat and simmer gently for about 10 minutes.
7. Add white wine and again bring mixture to just below boiling. Reduce heat and simmer for 10 minutes more.
8. Serve one fillet in each soup bowl, adding the broth.

> **HILTON-RICHFIELD**
> *Thicken this soup up, to make it a full-bodied winter dish, by adding cooked barley, left-over rice, or any left-over pasta. Cubed boiled potatoes left over also add to the body. If you use any of these, though, put them into the soup before the fish goes on top.*

Fresh Oyster Stew

INGREDIENTS:
32 freshly opened oysters, with their
 juice, removed from shell
dash of celery salt
60 mℓ sherry
10 mℓ paprika
120 g butter
10 mℓ Worcester sauce
250 mℓ milk
250 mℓ fresh cream

METHOD:
1. Place all the ingredients, except cream, milk and butter, in the top part of a double-boiler over boiling water. *Be careful not to let the base of the top part touch the water beneath it.*
2. Stir briskly for about 1 minute until oysters are just beginning to curl.
3. Add cream and milk and continue stirring until the mixture is just about to boil. *Do not allow to boil.*
4. Pour into hot soup plates. Serve piping hot with the remaining butter and sprinkle with paprika.

HILTON-RICHFIELD
This classic, simple oyster stew is ideal for fresh oysters, but which may be a day or two over the criterion for complete freshness. If the oysters have been kept in the fridge, and the shells are just beginning to open, or to show signs of opening by exuding their liquid, pop them into the pan for oyster stew. Once they do begin to open, though, it's a devil-may-care sort of person who'd take the risk of eating them raw, on the half-shell.

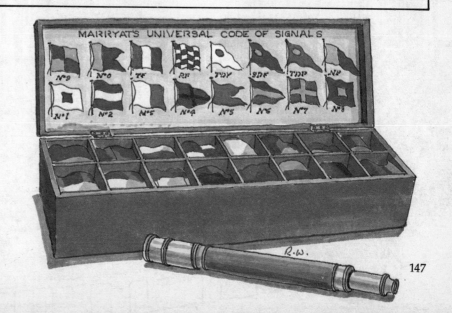

147

LINGER
LONGER

R. Ward '86

94 Juta Street,
Braamfontein, Johannesburg 2001
Telephone: (011) 339-2765
PO Box 31363, Braamfontein 2017
Closed Saturday lunch and Sundays
Fully licensed

Linger Longer

*B*en Filmalter, the owner, is one of the most experienced restaurateurs in the country: he knows the game inside out. The up-market Linger Longer is his own favourite enterprise, though, and he thoroughly enjoys the high reputation he has earned among gourmets. Part of this he owes, he is the first to admit, to master-chef Walter Ulz, who has been cooking classical French cuisine here for over 10 years. That must tell us something.

It's a beautiful restaurant, relaxing both to the eye and the body. The oldish house has been converted into a series of interleading rooms, each with its own character, and with a delightful ladies' bar adjoining. So many conversions of this kind can lead to poky discomfort, with bad routing of food from the kitchen causing waiters to bump into each other – and the furniture.

Not here! This is a thoroughgoing professional operation, that runs as smooth as silk even during the busiest service, and Mr Ulz is recognised by his colleagues in the profession as one of the finest cooks in the land. Longstanding customers with famous names agree. If you could wander discreetly through the rooms at any lunchtime, any dinner session, you would undoubtedly recognise faces from the upper echelons of Johannesburg society and the rarified upper strata of business.

Upstairs, it's another story. Here Mr Filmalter has created an entirely separate restaurant, "Leipoldt's". It's a simple, buffet service room with Cape Dutch-style cooking (adapted to modern tastes to some extent) forming the basis. Diners in a hurry can help themselves from steaming cauldrons, without spending a lot of money or time.

Downstairs at the Linger Longer, however, it would be wrong to expect cheapness, either in the kitchen or on your bill. This is high quality, and one pays accordingly. Not excessively, let it be said immediately, for we South Africans traditionally resent paying high prices for food in our own country. On the whole, the prices here are eminently reasonable, including what you pay for a marvellous selection of wines from the excellent cellar.

Fillets of Trout with Salmon Mousse

INGREDIENTS:
4 fresh rainbow trout
50 g fresh kingklip
80 g fresh salmon
125 m*l* cream
4 bunches baby spinach
a clove garlic
a few cooked shrimps
2 whole eggs
50 g butter
60 m*l* extra cream
a few cooked mussels
Hollandaise sauce (see "Standard
   Recipes")
1 *l* court-bouillon (see "Standard
   Recipes")
salt and seasoning

METHOD:
1. Cut the fresh salmon fillets and the kingklip fillets into pieces, and put into the liquidiser with 2 whole eggs. Add cream and seasoning and blend until all is creamy.
2. Skin the trout, leaving the heads on for the time being. Carefully fillet each fish, removing the backbone from the inside, and not cutting the top side open. Once the backbone is removed, cut the head away.
3. Stuff each trout with the salmon and kingklip mousse.
4. Butter some heavy-duty foil, place the four trout in it, one-on-one, seal, and poach in the court-bouillon for about 15 to 20 minutes.
5. Meanwhile, remove the stalks from the baby spinach. Melt the butter in a large pan, and sauté the spinach gently, adding (the extra 60 m*l*) cream and garlic. Check for seasoning and add salt and pepper to taste while cooking.
6. Place a bed of cooked spinach on your four serving plates. Undo the foil, remove the trout fillets and place them on the beds of spinach. Top with a few shelled mussels and shrimps. Cover everything with Hollandaise sauce and glaze under the grill. Serve very hot.

HILTON-RICHFIELD

Filleting trout is not as difficult as it sounds. In fact, it is one of the easier fish to fillet. If you are not sure, though, get your friendly neighbourhood professional chef to do the first two, while you do the next two under his stern gaze. Don't be shy to ask. Most chefs are only too delighted to show off their skills to us untutored amateurs. The only tricky bit in this recipe is cutting off the backbone with a pair of scissors or snippers, before you take the whole fillet off the head. Don't tell the chefs we suggested this, but we have found a pair of electrical side-cutters ideal for this little job!

If you have had to use frozen trout, this recipe is excellent, for it adds strong fishy tastes to the blandness of the trout's flesh.

Seafood Casserole with Whisky

INGREDIENTS:
4 crayfish tails, cut to bite size
4 langoustines (whole)
250 m*l* fresh salmon, cubed
4 large prawns, cleaned, deveined
250 m*l* kingklip fillet, cubed
8 mussels in shell
shrimps for decoration
50 g butter
5 m*l* fresh dill
500 m*l* fish fumet (see "Standard
    Recipes")
3 m*l* saffron threads
30 m*l* chopped onion
30 m*l* Scotch whisky
250 m*l* cream
salt and seasoning to taste

METHOD:
1. Heat the butter in a pan and sauté the
pieces of crayfish, the whole prawns and
langoustines with 30 m*l* chopped onion
and the saffron threads.
2. When partially cooked, heat the
whisky in a spoon, pour on and flame.

Now add the fish stock and simmer for 10
minutes.
3. Add the cubes of kingklip and
salmon, the mussels, the fresh dill and
cream, and simmer for another 5 minutes.
4. Remove to a casserole dish and decorate with cooked shrimps. Serve with
saffron rice.

HILTON-RICHFIELD
*Chef Walter Ulz gives the following
ingredients for his version of Saffron
Rice: 500 m*l* rice, a few threads of
saffron, 15 m*l* sautéed onion, salt
and seasoning. Cook it the way you
like best.*

  *Fresh salmon, meaning non-
frozen, Canadian or other northerly-
caught fish, is virtually
unobtainable. Frozen salmon can be
found here and there. Cape salmon
hasn't the same taste or texture as the
North Atlantic or Pacific varieties,
but it's an excellent substitute.*

73 Corlett Drive, Birnam,
Johannesburg 2196
Telephone: (011) 440-3775
Closed Saturday lunch and Sundays
Fully licensed

Lobster Hole

There are not many out-and-out speciality fish restaurants in the Transvaal. Until recently, the very idea would have been laughable, because of the irregularity of the supply of fresh fish.

The Lobster Hole is an exception to the rule. It has been here under the same ownership for many years and, no matter what the state of the market, the paucity of fish in the sea, or the reluctance of traders to bring the things up-country, the Lobster Hole has always had its supplies of crayfish, langoustines, prawns, oysters and fresh fish of every kind.

It hasn't been easy. The secret has been the owner's determination to have adequate supplies at all times. This meant building store-rooms of larger size and more sophisticated than most restaurants, and buying in very big bulk whenever the market allowed. This heavy buying at advantageous prices also meant that the restaurant could offer its seafood at prices far lower than average.

Of course, in the off-season, you can't expect to find a fresh rock lobster. Here, though, the preservation of the fish's quality has been so meticulously carried out that only a top gastronome could tell that the tail on his plate came from a frozen fish. And equal skill goes into the cooking of every dish offered.

There's a real undersea feel about this restaurant. Built on three levels, with the dimmest lighting, fish tanks swirling with multi-coloured denizens of the deep, the aromas of spices and herbs drifting in from the kitchen, you are put into the mood on arrival by a display on ice of most of the produce available each day.

The wines are reasonably priced and there's a good range of the rarer estates. The service is swift, skilled and friendly, and altogether the Lobster Hole is a most superior fish restaurant.

Shellfish a la Lobster Hole

INGREDIENTS:
4 fresh crayfish tails
4 king size prawns, deveined
4 medium size langoustines
4 canned artichoke hearts, drained and
   sliced
50 g onion, chopped
1 clove garlic, chopped
40 g tomato purée
75 g butter
75 mℓ fresh cream
rice cooked your own way
150 g mushrooms, sliced
2 canned celery hearts, sliced
50 g green peppers, chopped
3 mℓ mixed dried herbs
30 mℓ cognac or brandy
30 mℓ oil
200 mℓ fish fumet (see "Standard
   Recipes")

METHOD:
1. Remove the heads from langoustines
and prawns. Split the crayfish tails, still
in the shell. Split the langoustines and
prawns in two, lengthwise.
2. Heat the oil and butter together and
sauté the seafood in it, together with the
mushrooms, onion and green pepper,

until the shells turn red.
3. Season with the mixed herbs and
flame with the brandy. (Heat the brandy
first before pouring it over, and use a
match, so that it flames immediately.)
4. Moisten with the fish fumet, then add
the celery and artichoke, garlic, tomato
purée and fresh cream. Cook gently for
about 15 to 20 minutes, covered with a
lid.
5. Serve hot over a bed of rice.

HILTON-RICHFIELD
*Don't throw the langoustine heads
and prawn heads away, nor the
crayfish shells from the empty plates.
Be thrifty! Chop them up to save
space, and keep them tightly bagged
in your deep-freezer. One of these
days you can use them (with other
shells and heads you've rescued from
the rubbish bin) to make a bisque, or
to make a lobster sauce or flavour a
lobster butter. Of course, hotel and
restaurant kitchens never sink so
low as to do this (much!).*

Mussels "Marinière", Our Style

INGREDIENTS:
about 2,5 kg fresh mussels (about 600 g per person)
2 shallots or small onions, chopped
6 parsley stalks, chopped
30 g butter
150 mℓ milk
parsley, chopped (for garnish)
200 mℓ dry white wine
50 g large onion, chopped or sliced
2 cloves garlic, minced or crushed
25 g flour
50 mℓ fresh cream
freshly ground black pepper to taste

METHOD:
1. Prepare the mussels for cooking (see "Standard Recipes"). Put them in a saucepan or casserole, add the white wine, onions, shallots, garlic, parsley stalks and the black pepper. (No salt, as the sea-water in the mussels contains enough salt already.) Cook over a medium heat, stirring well so that all the mussels are equally cooked. When the shells are open and the liquid is about to overflow (when covered with a lid), they are ready. *Do not overcook or the mussels will become muscles!*

2. Drain the mussels and place them in individual serving bowls.
3. Pass the liquid in which they have been cooked through a cloth, and reserve. (Or put through fine sieve.)
4. Prepare a white roux (see "Standard Recipes") with the butter and flour. Moisten with the milk and the decanted cooking liquid, and work up into a smooth and creamy sauce. Add the cream and allow to thicken over a mild heat. Pour over the mussels and sprinkle with chopped parsley. Serve with French bread or thin, buttered brown bread.

HILTON-RICHFIELD
Don't risk using mussels someone has prised off the rocks. Stick to the delicious cultivated variety now freely available. When serving, don't forget the finger-bowls. You'll need them! And also bibs, or a plentiful supply of paper napkins. You must have a container to chuck the shells in. Why not do it the northern French way, by placing a couple of bins on the floor, between the guests, so that they can fling out the shells with a satisfying thwack! Peasant dishes call for peasant styles! Also, provide dessert spoons for slurping up the sauce.

Cor 7th Avenue and 3rd Avenue,
Parktown North, Johannesburg 2193
Telephone: (011) 880-1946
Closed Saturday lunch, Sunday evening,
and all day Monday
Wine & Malt licence

Ma Cuisine

A tiny restaurant in the best traditions of European family-run establishments. Mr and Mrs Jorn Pless are Danes. Their sous-chef, Christian, is also a skilled young Dane; so is their maîtresse d'hôtel.

The highly expert cooking, however, is in the true French tradition. Mr Pless worked for years in France, before he opened his own highly-respected restaurant in Copenhagen. Mrs Pless makes some of the finest pastry we have come across hereabouts.

Everything the kitchen cooks can be followed by the guests, for the finishing kitchen is glassed-in; so that if your conversation fades out on you, you and your partner can gaze fascinatedly at the process of turning out some of the finest French cooking in the city.

But the room is definitely Scandinavian in feel: everything light and bright and spotless; heavy white napery covering the tables; the simplest of wall decorations, with many menus from some of France's top restaurants.

By popular demand (in this case, a true phrase) Pless has included a few Scandinavian specialities on his menu, and at Sunday lunchtime, his advertised "Brunch" is the nearest thing to a true Danish "smorrebrod" you are ever likely to see south of the Equator.

Partner with Jorn Pless in this venture is the genial, ever-smiling, hail-fellow-well-met Graham Peaceful, a gourmet and wine expert and member of the National Committee of the Chaîne des Rôtisseurs. It is a pleasure to record that a restaurant of this high quality is actually doing very well in these difficult times.

Gravad Laks, Danish Style

INGREDIENTS:
2 sides Canadian Red Springer salmon
(about 800 g each). (Cape salmon or,
better still, 74, will do just as well)
20 g crushed white peppercorns
750 mℓ salt
750 mℓ sugar
plenty of fresh dill

METHOD:
1. Clean and scale the fish, and dry in a dishcloth. (Your fishmonger will remove the backbone).
2. Mix the sugar, salt and white pepper and rub into the fish, but not on the skin side (it will not be absorbed).
3. Place one side of fish on a flat dish, skin side down. Cover the surface with chopped dill. Place the other side of fish over it, skin side up. Sprinkle whole plate with chopped dill.
4. Take a wooden tray, or a breadboard, long enough to cover the fish (or nearly), place it on top, and weigh it down with a brick. Hold in the refrigerator for 48 hours.
5. Separate the two sides and scrape off the salt mixture that has not been absorbed, with the back of a knife. Slice thinly, as with smoked salmon, and serve with toast and dill sauce.

DILL SAUCE:
1 bunch dill, chopped fine
dash cognac to taste
sugar to taste
500 mℓ crème fraîche (see below)
125 mℓ Dijon mustard
salt and pepper to taste

METHOD:
1. Mix crème fraîche and mustard, salt, pepper and a little sugar. Add cognac to taste.
2. Finish with chopped dill and leave in refrigerator. (You can use the dill left over from covering the salmon.)

CREME FRAICHE:
1 ℓ fresh cream
250 mℓ buttermilk

Blend well, leave at room temperature for 24 hours, then in the fridge for 24 hours.

NOTE: If you make the crème fraîche and the dill sauce at the same time as you prepare the gravad laks, everything will be ready at the same time.

HILTON-RICHFIELD
A noble treatment of a good, firm fish, beloved throughout Scandinavia and northern Germany. The Pless family are from Denmark: Jorn's restaurant there was very well known. There are other versions of gravad laks, but this one is as authentically Danish as smørrebrød itself.

Turbot à la Vinaigrette de Tomate

(Rock cod or kabeljou are excellent substitutes)

INGREDIENTS:

4 x 200 g pieces of fish
50 mℓ olive oil
10 mℓ fresh tarragon, chopped, or 3 mℓ
    dried
a few chives, snipped
2 finely chopped shallots (or small
    onions)
2 bunches baby spinach
300 mℓ fish fumet (see "Standard
    Recipes")
50 mℓ tarragon vinegar
10 mℓ fresh chervil, chopped, or 3 mℓ
    dried
10 mℓ fresh thyme, chopped, or 3 mℓ
    dried
6 red, ripe tomatoes, blanched, peeled,
    seeded
salt and pepper to taste

METHOD:

1. In a saucepan place 150 mℓ of fish fumet together with the olive oil and the
tarragon vinegar. Heat until it just starts
to thicken.
2. Beat in the chopped herbs, onion and
the coarsely chopped tomato.
3. Place the rest of the fish fumet in a
shallow saucepan and poach the fish
fillets in it for 2 minutes.
4. Prepare the baby spinach, either
steamed, blanched or sweated in butter,
and dress it on a serving plate.
5. Dress the fish fillets on top of the spinach, and garnish all with the tomato
vinaigrette mixture.

HILTON-RICHFIELD

If you have to substitute dried herbs for fresh, use one-quarter the quantity. Some authorities recommend half the quantity, but we find this often makes the dish too herby. Spinach is an underrated vegetable. There are so many ways of preparing it. Here's one of our own: Let a bunch of spinach sweat in its own juice until nearly, but not quite, soft enough to eat. Remove, put in a colander and press out excess moisture with a wooden spoon. Chop finely or put in a blender (but this purées it too thinly). Chop an onion, fry it very brown, drain, chop again and mix with the spinach. Chop a hard-boiled egg and mix with the rest. Stir in a tiny quantity of bacon fat, chicken or duck fat, or some other rich fat. Flatten out into a serving dish and put under the grill. When surface becomes a little dark and crispy, remove and sprinkle more chopped hard-boiled egg over it. Cut in slices, as you would Italian "polenta".

Umhlanga Sands Hotel ★★★ TYYY
Umhlanga Rocks, Natal 4320
Telephone: (031) 51-2300
PO Box 223, Umhlanga Rocks 4320
Open Monday to Saturday, evenings only
Fully licensed

Mayflower

While all over the country the hotel business suffers depression and blues, and while there's much moaning at the bar (and in the office), it's an eye-opener to walk into the Umhlanga Sands Hotel and see the foyer teeming with people, dressed in their casuals, in swimwear, in summery dresses, and to find that the place is invariably 90 percent full.

You nod in comprehension when you realise that this is a time-sharing enterprise, one of the most successful Southern Sun operations in the country. We don't know what your conception of time-sharing is, but ours took a knock when we found the Mayflower Restaurant in this excellent resort hotel.

However the visitors decide to feed themselves during their holiday here, it is obvious that they want at least one or two meals of a high standard, and The Mayflower certainly obliges. The executive responsible for the theme and the decoration of this room deserves a good pat on the back.

There isn't a replica of the actual ship that took the Pilgrim Fathers to the shores of the New World, but there are models of other ships of the times – worth a detailed stury, incidentally – and on the back of the menu is printed a list of the names of all the original families who braved the cruel sea to find a new life in America.

You don't have to be a resident to enjoy the comforts of this fine restaurant, of course. The cooking is good, the service suave and efficient and the prices manageable by any budget. Altogether a splendid example of Southern Sun's revitalised catering policy.

Shrimp Curry "Vasco Da Gama"

INGREDIENTS:
500 g shrimps, frozen
5 mℓ – 10 mℓ chilli powder
45 mℓ tomato paste
50 g butter
2 large onions, chopped
¼ bunch curry leaves
30 g tamarind, soaked in 30 mℓ hot
   water, then strained
rice, cooked
5 large tomatoes, blanched, skinned,
   seeded, chopped coarsely into a
   "concassé"
½ bunch fresh coriander (dhunia)
salt and pepper to taste

METHOD:
1. Melt the butter in a pan. Gently sauté
the onions, garlic and chilli powder. Add
the curry leaves and the tomato concassé, and sauté until soft.
2. Add the tomato paste, tamarind, salt
and pepper. Add the shrimps and cook
slowly, for about 5 minutes. Check seasoning.
3. Serve in china bowl and garnish with
sprigs of fresh coriander (also known as
Chinese parsley). Serve rice separately.

HILTON-RICHFIELD
*Readers outside Natal won't find
curry leaves and tamarind all that
easily. They aren't essential, of
course, but they certainly do make a
vivid difference to the taste of any
Indian-style dish. Tamarind is sold in
blocks in most Indian shops. In
Johannesburg, you'll find some at the
Oriental Plaza in Fordsburg or at
Akhalwaya's spice shop at 45a Bree
Street: curry leaves, too. Otherwise,
ask your Durban connections to send
you some.*

   *Tamarind should always be soaked
in a little hot water before using.
Strain, but never press the seeds.
They're hairy and have a nasty habit
of leaving horrid and annoying bits
in the mouth.*

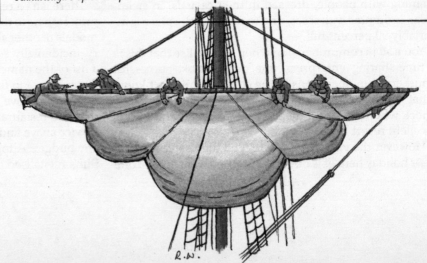

Sea Goddess Salad

(For 2 people)

INGREDIENTS:
1 large iceberg lettuce or 2 butter
   lettuce
250 g shrimps (frozen, or fresh),
   deveined, shelled and simmered in a
   court-bouillon (see "Standard
   Recipes"), left to cool in the liquid
2 slices bread cut into 1 cm cubes,
   roasted golden-brown in butter
100 g fresh sliced white mushrooms
2 tomatoes, cut into quarters
1 small bunch parsley, chopped
DRESSING:
250 mℓ fresh cream
1 clove garlic, chopped
5 ml Worcester sauce
8 anchovy fillets, chopped
juice of 1 or 2 lemons
chopped parsley
1 onion, chopped
salt, white ground pepper

METHOD FOR DRESSING:
1. Pour the lemon juice into a bowl with
the Worcester sauce. Pour in the cream
and whisk.

2. Add in the rest of the ingredients.
Blend well. Check seasoning.
3. Place a portion of cooked shrimps on
each serving plate. Cover with the sauce.
Place the lettuce at each side, the mushrooms over the lettuce, tomatoes on the
side, croûtons and parsley scattered over
the whole.

HILTON-RICHFIELD
A very pretty luncheon salad for a hot summer's day. Anchovy fillets enhance the taste of any sauce to accompany seafood or fish. The Umhlanga Sands Hotel, incidentally, is a time-share establishment, though of course the restaurant is open to all. Those who have reservations about time-sharing should visit this hotel; it's packed to the eaves almost every day of the year.

Metropole Hotel ★★★ TYYY
38 Long Street, Cape Town 8001
Telephone: (021) 23-6363
PO Box 3086, Cape Town 8000
Open daily
Fully licensed

The Metropole

We have known the Metropole for four decades, certainly all the time that the Bowman family have owned it. The tradition of solid food, well-cooked, well-served, well-presented, was carried on by the late Harold Bowman and is being maintained with skill and enthusiasm by his sons.

Somehow, for some reason, the fish at the Metropole always seems to be fresher, tastier, more straight-out-of-the-ocean than anywhere else. This might just be illusion; on the other hand, it might be due to the Bowman brothers' network of connections in the trade (and, we suspect, with a few private fishermen) that ensures a never-faltering supply of products of the sea.

Never resting on their reputation, the Bowmans frequently present speciality seasons, during which one type of fish is prominently featured. It may be prawns, or perlemoen, or snoek, or crayfish: it could be oysters or clams. Whatever they choose to promote, you can be assured of remarkably good value for money both in the seafood on offer and in the wines recommended as accompaniment.

And perhaps it's that feature, more than any other, that keeps the room chock-a-block full in these difficult times. Certainly The Metropole deserves its continuing success. We know people who, in fact, telephone from Johannesburg to reserve a table. Not many restaurants can boast a fan-club like that!

When we asked Brian Bowman for two recipes for this book, with typical enthusiasm he offered us half-a-dozen, every one of them worth printing for you. There's space, regretfully, for only two. Fancy cookery is not the theme at the Metropole, however: this is the home of seafood prepared with simplicity and skill, honestly, interestingly and impressively. (People do ask for their meat dishes, too, of course, and they are not disappointed.)

LM Prawns à la Metropole

Served with savoury rice

INGREDIENTS:
40 medium LM prawns ("Star 5")
juice of 1 lemon
125 g margarine (not butter, which
** burns too easily)**
1 clove garlic, crushed
THE SAVOURY RICE:
1 ℓ cooked rice (4 cups)
1 small can red pimiento, chopped
50 g margarine
250 mℓ cooked fresh green peas
250 mℓ button mushrooms, chopped

METHOD:
1. The prawns: Cut prawns in halves lengthwise and devein. Wash them and dry on paper towels.
2. Melt margarine in pan, then add the crushed garlic and lemon juice. Place prawns in pan, the cut-side down, and simmer until the shells start to turn red.
3. Serve on a bed of savoury rice with side servings of garlic butter or peri-peri sauce.

THE SAVOURY RICE:
4. Heat margarine in a large pan. Place cooked rice, peas, pimiento and mushrooms in pan and fry, stirring often, over medium heat, until golden-brown.

THE GARNISH:
chopped parsley
8 slices lemon
20 canned black olives, cut in halves

Chop the parsley finely and sprinkle on prawns. Place a half-olive on each prawn and a slice of lemon on each side of the plate.

HILTON-RICHFIELD
So simple, no mess, no bother, no time-consuming preparation! Perhaps this is why the customers have been coming back to the Metropole for prawns (and all their other excellent fish dishes) for decades, and why, when the Bowman brothers run a prawn promotion, the place packs out. Incidentally, the term is still "LM" prawns, it seems. They'll never get people to say "Maputo prawns" — it just doesn't sound right, does it?

Perlemoen Kedgeree

INGREDIENTS:

5 medium-sized perlemoen (buy perlemoen already removed from shell and scrub them clean with a pot-scourer)
1 large onion, sliced finely
2 large boiled potatoes, diced
3 mℓ powdered nutmeg (or grated)
rice cooked your own way
125 g margarine (not butter, as butter burns easily)
1 tin whole, peeled tomatoes, diced
1 clove garlic, crushed
3 mℓ cinnamon powder
chopped parsley
salt and pepper to taste

METHOD:

1. Cook the perlemoen whole in a pressure cooker at highest pressure for 20 minutes.
2. Cut perlemoen into quarters and mince together with the onion and garlic.
3. Melt margarine into a pan. Add all ingredients and sauté for 10 minutes.
4. Serve on a bed of rice and garnish with chopped parsley.

HILTON-RICHFIELD

We had always been put off from using perlemoen because of the tales we had heard about the difficulty of cooking it. There's no doubt this is the easiest way we've come across, though it does mean mincing the fish. Serving perlemoen as "abalone", the Chinese and Californian way in thin slices, takes a gread deal more time and trouble, for the darn thing is nearly always so rubbery. We have even bought some canned abalone (Chinese labelled, Hermanus produced!) that was disastrous. You could have soled a pair of shoes with it.

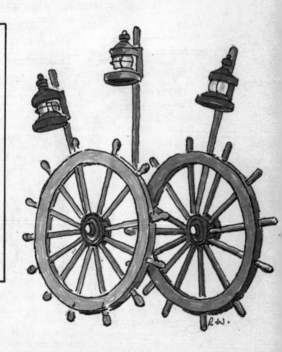

Mount Nelson Hotel ★ ★ ★ ★ ★ TYYY
76 Orange Street, Gardens,
Cape Town 8001
Telephone: (021) 23-1000
PO Box 2608, Cape Town 8000
Open daily
Fully licensed

Mount Nelson Grill

There are so many metaphors that suit the Nellie! Even that vulgar diminutive of its name carries affection and respect. The Queen of South African hotels . . . the Rock of Gibraltar . . . a Stately Home of England transplanted to the Cape . . . Buckingham Palace by the Sea . . . a famous old hotel that takes its place alongside the Peninsula in Hong Kong, Gleneagles in Scotland, Raffles in Singapore, the Savoy in London, as one of the world's great hostelries.

For many decades the custom of "wintering at the Cape" among the titled and wealthy of Britain meant only one thing: a sojourn at the Mount Nelson.

It must be admitted, however, that over the past few years the Nellie's reputation for food suffered a little. In local circles it was thought to be very ordinary, unimaginative, even stodgy. A change in management, though, has brought about a vibrant uplift in the food in both the Garden Room (which offers table d'hôte fare) and the Grill Room, which has regained its place as one of Cape Town's major venues for a grand night out.

The menu is still international grillroom fare, of course: it would be silly to expect anything else. The quality of the cooking and the service, the richness of the surroundings, the traditional values of five-star hotel entertaining, are all here, and the overall performance is impressive indeed.

It's very pleasant for us, who have always admired the Mount Nelson, even in its less glowing days, to be able to say that those first-paragraph metaphors are still true. The Nellie is Queen of 'Em All.

169

Curried Crayfish

INGREDIENTS:
4 whole crayfish
2 bay leaves
15 ml curry powder
3 medium tomatoes, blanched, skinned, deseeded and chopped
4 portions cooked rice
2 medium onions, diced
3 cloves garlic, crushed
15 m1 masala powder
100 ml fish stock (see "Standard Recipes")
4 portions cooked peas
salt and pepper to taste

METHOD:
1. Boil crayfish for 10 minutes. Cut into halves, clean and wash. Cut each half into 5 or 6 pieces.
2. Fry onions, tomatoes, garlic in oil. Add curry powder and masala, and the bay leaves.
3. Add seasoned crayfish pieces and fry slowly for 6 to 8 minutes.
4. Add fish stock and simmer for 4 to 5 minutes.
5. Arrange in large deep dish and serve with rice and peas.

HILTON-RICHFIELD
As simple and easy a recipe for curry as you'll ever come across. There's a wide choice of curry powders and masalas on the shelves but, if you can, go to the local Indian market, where there's certain to be a specialist shop making up their own masalas and curries. Incidentally, we often notice a little confusion between "masala" and "Marsala". They're pronounced the same. "Masala" is the Indian spice mixture, while "Marsala" is the sweet wine from Sicily, indispensable to a proper "zabaglione".

The Autumn sun sets over Nederburg in the Paarl Valley.

Imagine a wine that embodies the warmth, richness and intensity of a vineyard aglow.

A mature, full-bodied wine
with a rich, late summer texture.

From the Winemasters.

Nederburg

Edelrood

BERRY BUSH NEW 1715E

We'd like to share Nederburg with you.
Call us at (02211) 623104 to arrange your visit.

Seafood Platter à la Maison

INGREDIENTS:

2 crayfish, 500 g – 600 g each
500 g filleted kabeljou
8 prawns
200 g fillet of kingklip (for fish fingers)
100 g whitebait, frozen
200 g calamari rings
100 g butter
2 cloves garlic, crushed
2 lemons
100 g breadcrumbs
dash Worcester sauce
2 eggs
4 portions cooked rice
200 mℓ oil
2 medium tomatoes, skinned, deseeded and chopped
50 g flour
50 mℓ milk
parsley for garnish
pinch paprika
4 portions cooked peas
dash lemon juice
salt and pepper to taste

METHOD:

1. Boil the crayfish in salted water for 10 minutes. Cool and cut in halves, wash crayfish and place on tray for grilling. Place a few flakes of butter on each crayfish half and grill for 4 to 5 minutes.

2. Cut the kabeljou fillet into 4 equal slices, season with salt, pepper, Worcester sauce and lemon juice. Dust with flour and fry in butter and half the oil, mixed, for 3 or 4 minutes each side.

3. Fry calamari rings in hot oil for 2 minutes. Add 2 crushed cloves of garlic and the tomatoes. Cook slowly for 5 minutes.

4. Cut kingklip fillets into fish fingers, about 17 mm thick. Season with salt, pepper, Worcester sauce, lemon juice. Dust with flour, pull through beaten egg and roll in breadcrumbs. Fry gently.

5. Cut open prawns, clean out, wash, season with a little salt, pepper, Worcester sauce, lemon juice. Place on tray with little oil and grill.

6. Defrost whitebait, wash, soak in milk, dust with flour and deep-fry in hot oil for 1 minute. Shake oil off and season with salt and paprika.

7. Arrange everything on large platter, garnish with lemon and parsley. Serve rice and peas separately.

MOUNT NELSON CHEF SAYS:
This is not a particularly simple and certainly not a cheap dish for the housewife to prepare, especially if she has to go to the fish market or the local fishmonger to get everything together. But it does mean that it could become your special "house recipe". If you do not like the fish fried, then poach or grill it. If there is no kabeljou available, use hake or yellowtail instead.

HILTON-RICHFIELD

Unfortunately, there's nothing you can substitute for whitebait. The tiny, frozen or fresh anchovies prepared locally are the same size and even look like whitebait, but there the resemblance ends. They're strong-tasting and very pervasive, more suitable to a fish casserole than to a dish of this nature. Therefore, if you can't find the proper English whitebait in your local freezer-counter, omit them. (Mariner's Wharf in Hout Bay have them.)

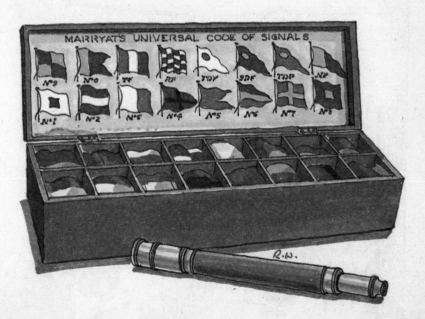

173

Hyde Square, Jan Smuts Avenue,
Hyde Park, Johannesburg 2196
Telephone: (011) 788-4115
Open daily
Fully licensed

Oasis

What is the most common single complaint you hear about our South African restaurants? We should imagine it was inconsistency: a good meal one day, an indifferent one the next. Undoubtedly this is true of some restaurants, and this is not the time to go into the reasons.

The accusation could never be made, however, about the Oasis. For 20 years now, this family-run dining-room has been serving consistently good food to the citizens of Johannesburg's northern suburbs. The only serious change has been in the décor, which underwent a metamorphosis in mid-1986.

The decoration of the room, let's be honest, was never a strong point. It was ordinary, to use a kind word. Of course, the customers who come back here year after year for the solid, satisfying cooking don't worry about what's on the walls.

The second generation of the owning family did, though, and after a few years apprenticeship with Southern Sun Hotels (from which he emerged with a brilliant record) young Nic Georgades persuaded Dad and Mum that the time had come to modernise.

Perhaps "modernise" isn't the right word, for the Oasis now is a striking example of Art Deco style – that somewhat self-conscious but very pleasing combination of shadowy figures, pastel colours and outré outlines that dominated the 1920s and 1930s in Europe. It works delightfully well here. The room is airy, pleasant, colourful – and the change has put a zip back into the service, which is meticulously correct.

The cooking hasn't changed, however, and let's be thankful for that. It's principally middle-of-the-road Continental style, with the odd dish here and there from the owners' native Greece. Two such recipes contribute a fine exotic touch to this book.

175

Mediterranean Meze

INGREDIENTS:
160 g chicken livers, cleaned
240 g baby calamari, cut into 3 mm
  wide rings
2 large onions, finely chopped
15 mℓ tomato purée
pinch mixed herbs
2 anchovy fillets
Kalamata olives
taramasalata (if available)
200 mℓ oil
6 ripe tomatoes
5 mℓ peri-peri sauce, or to taste
Feta cheese
juice of 1 lemon
seasoned flour
100 g butter
pepper and salt

METHOD:
CHICKEN LIVERS:
1. Blanch the livers in boiling salted water for 3 minutes. Strain and refresh in cold water.
2. Blanch, peel and deseed the tomatoes. Chop into a "concassé" (that simply means "chop coarsely"). Add the chopped onions and then the tomato purée.

3. Transfer the concassé mixture to a skillet over a low heat. When it simmers, add the herbs and the livers. Continue to simmer for about 5 minutes.
4. Add the peri-peri sauce and seasoning to taste.

CALAMARI:
5. Shake the calamari rings in seasoned flour in a plastic bag. Remove and shake off excess flour.
6. Heat the oil in a deep saucepan and fry the calamari rings for about 3 minutes, until golden-brown. Remove and drain on kitchen paper.
7. Now brown the butter in a skillet, and cook the calamari again: This time simply toss them in the butter, adding the juice of a lemon at the last minute.

GARNISH:
8. Arrange the cooked livers, whole, on a large hors d'oeuvre plate, to one side. Place the cooked calamari at the other side.
9. Garnish with 2 anchovy fillets, sliced Feta cheese and a spoonful of taramasalata (optional). Finish with a sprig of parsley and some olives.

HILTON-RICHFIELD
Real taramasalata is hard to find, so is the beautiful smoked cod's roe from Scotland that used to be readily available. Thrupps, that lovely shop in Rosebank in Johannesburg, usually has cod's roe and some Greek delicatessens stock a decent tarama. There are some spurious concoctions in some of the supermarkets, albeit with Greek-sounding manufacturers' names, but they're nothing like the real thing, either in taste or appearance. An excellent substitution for the garnish in this case might be some smoked salmon pâté.

Prawns Turkolimano

INGREDIENTS:
32 shelled, deveined prawns
200 g Feta cheese
10 ml white wine
100 ml cream
200 g rice, prepared your own way
60 g butter
500 g tomato concassé (with chopped
   onion and tomato purée . . . see
   previous recipe)
5 cloves garlic, chopped
10 ml brandy
1 bunch parsley, chopped
50 ml cooking oil

METHOD:
1. Deep-fry the prawns in oil. Remove and drain on paper.
2. In a pan, sauté garlic in butter until the aroma escapes.
3. Add the prawns to the garlic butter and toss in a pan for one or two minutes.
4. Add brandy, and flame.
5. Add the tomato concassé mixture and white wine. Allow to simmer for 10 minutes.
6. Remove from heat. Place the prawns in an ovenproof dish. Pour cream over the prawns. Sprinkle crumbled Feta cheese over the prawns and place under the grill.
7. Serve when the cheese has melted and browned. Sprinkle with chopped parsley.
8. Turn the cooked rice into savoury rice by your own favourite method. Serve this separately.

> ### HILTON-RICHFIELD
> *This is very much an eastern Mediterranean dish. If your tastes do not run to all that cooked tomato, cut down on the concassé and chop up a bunch of sweet basil instead. There's nothing that can substitute for the delicious aroma of that grilling cheese, though!*

On The Rocks

45 Stadler Road,
Blouberg Strand
Cape Town 7441
Telephone: (021) 52-2423
PO Box 202, Milnerton 7435
Closed Sunday evening and Mondays
Fully licensed

What a delightful triple-meaning name! Luckily, one of them (the impecunious one) doesn't apply here. The chink of ice in your glass is fairly represented at the bar in this pleasant room, and the situation is fairly and squarely right on the rocks, with the waves breaking almost over the picture windows.

This must be the most spectacular site for a restaurant in the Cape. You get the feeling that you could almost fish from the door – and possibly you could, but the authorities would not be pleased if you broke their laws and collected any of the giant crayfish or fat mussels that abound: they're protected.

Maryanne Maas, charming and efficient daughter of the late Pieter, runs the room in a way her dad would have approved of entirely. There's a big menu of both fish and meat dishes but, as one might expect at this seashore establishment, fish predominates. In fact, as much of three-quarters of all dishes cooked in the very modern and well-designed kitchen are the fresh fish that come in three or four times a week.

As with the other Maas restaurant, the Wooden Bridge at Milnerton, the wine list represents a fair selection of standard and estate wines, at prices even lower than the prevailingly low figures that appear on most lists at the Cape.

If enjoying good food – while enjoying the closest view of Robben Island that most law-abiding citizens ever manage – appeals to you and if you don't demand fancy presentations, fancy names and fancy prices, On The Rocks should be on your short list of restaurants to frequent.

Fillet of Kingklip "Roberto"

INGREDIENTS:
1,2 kg filleted kingklip
1 ℓ court-bouillon (see "Standard
    Recipes")
200 g shelled walnuts
¼ clove garlic, crushed
500 g spinach ribbon noodles
500 mℓ fish velouté (see "Standard
    Recipes")
15 mℓ paprika
30 g butter

METHOD:
1. Cook the spinach noodles in a large pot with plenty of vigorously boiling water. Time will depend on the thickness of the noodles – usually about 12 to 15 minutes. Test for softness. If preferred "al dente" (see note below), remove from heat earlier. Transfer to a colander and hold under the running cold water tap for a few seconds.
2. Cut the kingklip fillets into finger-sized strips. Pour the court-bouillon into a flat pan and bring to the boil. Carefully place the kingklip fingers in the liquid, and poach until cooked through.
3. In another pan, melt the butter with a little crushed garlic. Do not allow to over-heat. Place the cooked noodles in the butter and toss until all are coated. Place in the serving dish.
4. Place the fish on top of the noodles. Coat with the fish velouté, which should have been warmed, but not enough to cook it further.
5. Just before serving, sprinkle with the walnuts and paprika.

HILTON-RICHFIELD

Most South Africans prefer their pasta to be soft to the palate, while Italians like theirs "al dente" – firm enough to be bitten by the teeth. Consequently, nearly all our Italian restaurants overcook their pasta and you have to ask to get it done the Italian way. Nuts always add a touch of interest to a dish, whether sweet or savoury. Pecans will do here, of course, but if you want to go a little mad, use roasted pistachios – the undyed variety, if you can find them at less than R30 per kg. They're incredibly expensive these days. We wonder if anyone has ever tried growing pistachios in South Africa?

Mussels "On the Rocks"

INGREDIENTS:
24 fresh mussels, in the shell
2 crayfish tails
200 g flour
200 g white breadcrumbs
200 mℓ oil
4 cocktail gherkins
3 eggs
400 mℓ fish velouté (see "Standard
   Recipes")
4 toothpicks
salt, pepper, paprika to taste

METHOD:
1. Steam mussels over a double-boiler, or in a colander over boiling water. When they have opened (discard any that do not open), remove the flesh from the shells and remove the beards.
2. Toss the mussels in seasoned flour (flour with 5 mℓ each of salt, pepper and paprika), then dip into a bowl of beaten eggs, and finally in a dish of bread-crumbs.
3. Steam the crayfish tails in a colander over a pot of boiling water. Remove flesh from the shell, reserving the tail fins for garnish.
4. Slice crayfish tails into four equal portions. Arrange in centre of a snail dish, or any other suitable serving plate. (A proper snail dish is best, because the mussels fit into the indentations where the snails usually go.)
5. Heat the oil in a pan and shallow-fry the coated mussels on both sides until browned. Place them in the snail holes.
6. Coat the crayfish with fish velouté and serve.

BUTTERFLY GARNISH:
Stick a toothpick right through a gherkin, at the top, forming a kind of letter "T". Take two of the fins from the crayfish tail, and stick them on the end of the toothpick. Place one on each plate.

HILTON-RICHFIELD
The fresh mussels coming regularly these days from Maricult's Seafarm on the West Coast are so excellent, it seems a shame to cook them this way. But, on second thoughts, this is a clever recipe, for it dresses up the fish without adding strong flavours to the mussels. If anyone knows of a better way to serve mussels (or any small items of similar size) than on a snail dish, we'd like to know about it.

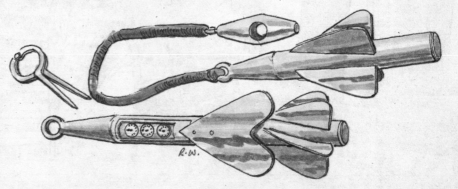

R. Ward '86

Oyster Box Hotel ★★★ TYYY
2 Lighthouse Road,
Umhlanga Rocks 4320
Telephone: (031) 51-2233
PO Box 22, Umhlanga Rocks 4320
Open daily
Fully licensed

Oyster Box

*T*his lovely hotel was here long before the giants erected their multi-storeyed caravanserais along the Umhlanga Rocks seafront. In fact, the Oyster Box is the doyen of hotels hereabouts and virtually the singlehanded founder of the resort's flourishing tourist trade.

Don't let this mislead you into believing that it's old-fashioned, fuddy-duddy or anything less than supremely efficient. Comfortable, of course, and furnished in the style of a country tweed, rather than a sharp, tailor-made, sharkskin, gent's natty suiting.

Inside, it's beautiful. That curving staircase from the foyer is unique in South Africa, and it sets the tone for the elegance of the entire establishment. "Establishment", we rather think, is the correct and proper term for the Oyster Box. No raucous music here, no fast foods, and a proper attention to the needs and wants of the weary guest. It's a lovely, restful place: a home from home.

The food is exactly right for the ambience. It's not "haute cuisine", and no wild flights of fancy appear on the menus. It is well-planned, painstakingly prepared, pleasantly presented and served in the style and to the standard we have come to expect of Natal. The fish dishes are particularly good: some imagination has certainly gone into their creation.

True to its name, the Oyster Box nearly always has fresh Natal wild oysters: not purchased from some casual fisherman or from a wholesaler, but plucked fresh daily from the hotel's own beds. They are quite simply marvellous: equal to the best South Africa has to offer.

Every day, too, fresh linefish appears, depending on what the catch has been like. No doubt the hotel has its own private arrangements with individual anglers, even possibly with King Neptune himself, and the guests have never been let down yet.

183

Sole Oyster Box

INGREDIENTS:

4 soles, about 400 g each, cleaned and filleted
24 fresh oysters
150 g cooked shrimps
3 mℓ cayenne pepper
dash lemon juice
125 mℓ white sauce
salt and pepper to taste
5 mℓ paprika
300 mℓ fresh cream
500 mℓ fish stock (see "Standard Recipes")
15 mℓ dry white wine
mashed potato and hard-boiled egg for garnish

METHOD:

1. Remove heads and skins of soles. (Add these to your store of fish stock.) Fillet the soles carefully and roll up the fillets from the tail end. A toothpick can be used to keep the rolls intact.
2. Chop the oysters and shrimps finely. Keep the fluid from the oysters in a dish, as it is very tasty.
3. Put the chopped oysters and shrimps in a small pot. Add the fluid from the oysters as well as the strained fish stock. Add the wine and lemon juice. Reduce by about one-half by boiling rapidly. *Reduce heat*.
4. Add the cream slowly and stir with a wooden spoon.
5. Poach the fillets of sole in this fish stock, and at the end add the dry white wine.
6. Serve the fillets in a large dish, covered with the sauce. Pipe mashed potato around the edge of the dish. Chop two hard-boiled eggs into the mashed potato for a pleasant effect.

184

HILTON-RICHFIELD

Two dozen fresh oysters to cook a sole dish for four people? How many people do you know who can afford to add an amount like R16 or R18 to the cost of a dish? It's all right for the Oyster Box in Umhlanga: they've got their own exclusive oyster beds where they pick them fresh every day. So they don't have to go traipsing along to the fishmongers to see if there are any fresh 'uns in today. And, of course, they're a lot fresher and a great deal cheaper than any you or we can buy!

Crayfish Brunetière

INGREDIENTS:
4 fresh crayfish
15 ml brandy
100 g butter
raw oysters for garnish
mashed potato for "anchoring"
250 ml crayfish sauce (see "Standard
   Recipes")
100 ml fresh cream
125 ml dry white wine
grated Parmesan cheese
little extra butter for the oysters
salt and pepper to taste

METHOD:
1. Remove the flesh from the crayfish shells, discarding the intestine and the coral. Cut the flimsy lower part of the shell away from the back part, so that the upturned back part can be used for serving.
2. Cut the crayfish meat into cubes.
3. Melt the butter in a pan. Braise the crayfish meat gently for about 2 minutes, being careful not to burn it.
4. Warm the brandy in a soup spoon, add it to the crayfish in the butter, and flame it (use a match to light it). Before the flame has had time to die down, smother it with lobster sauce. Stir. Add the wine and cream slowly and allow to simmer for about 15 minutes. Add salt and pepper to taste.
5. Remove the flesh from 8 oysters. Lightly fry them in a pan with just a little butter, and a sprinkling of Parmesan cheese. Cook only until they become opaque.
6. Serve the crayfish in the empty tail shells that have been "anchored" in individual plates with a little mashed potato. Garnish with two oysters on each, sprinkle with Parmesan cheese, and gratinate under the salamander or a hot grill.

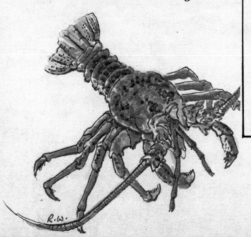

HILTON-RICHFIELD

Unfortunately, nothing really takes the place of genuine Parmigiano cheese from Italy. The Argentinian parmesan is nothing to write home about, while the locally made parmesan is pretty poor stuff. For taste, a good Emmenthaler or Gruyère is a fair substitute, (though not the Austrian-made ones: avoid them) and you have to let these cheeses get pretty stale before they will grate easily to a powder. Very thin flakes will do, though, made with your grater or on a mandoline. If you don't have a mandoline, that very useful kitchen tool, off to your nearest kitchen shop and have a look at one. Every French housewife has a mandoline. It pre-dates the food processor (which was also invented in France) by about 150 years.

Rosebank Hotel ★★★★ TYYY
Tyrwhitt Avenue, Rosebank,
Johannesburg 2196
Telephone: (011) 788-1820
PO Box 52025, Saxonwold 2132
Open daily
Fully licensed

Parktown

This is the principal restaurant of the four-star Rosebank Hotel, one of the most successful hostelries in the South African hotel firmament.

Not too big to be called impersonal, not too small for the term "cosy", the Rosebank fits exactly into the requirements of the commercial visitor, and the holiday-maker, too. When other hotels in Johannesburg appear to be suffering, the Rosebank is always comfortably patronised, with visitors both from home and overseas.

The Parktown is a well-planned and well-furnished room. Touches of formality, touches of lightness. Your surroundings are austere enough to announce that the meal is going to be seriously cooked and served, and relaxed enough to allow you to sit back and enjoy it all.

There are adequate facilities for the man in a hurry, or who doesn't want to spend a great deal. The carvery and buffet cater for him splendidly. And there is a full menu of classical French and other specialities, planned, cooked and presented by Jean-Pierre Siegenthaler.

Mr Siegenthaler, from Alsace-Lorraine in France, is a master of his profession, and a great stalwart of the South African Chefs Association. His kitchen runs like clockwork – it has to, for besides the high class à la carte food of the Parktown, it has to provide banqueting catering for the always busy function rooms of the hotel. But this is a thoroughgoing professional operation, and seated in the deep comfort of the Parktown's chairs, you will be aware only of the meticulous service and the excellence of the food.

Filet de Truite Saumonée à la Mousse de Poireaux St-Jacques

INGREDIENTS:
2 x 600 g Atlantic salmon-trout, filleted
200 g queen scallops
30 g rice
100 ml water (approximately)
4 small shallots (or small onions) chopped
400 ml cream
a little extra butter
300 g young leeks, washed, sliced
50 g butter, very cold
200 ml dry white wine
4 puff pastry fleurons
salt and pepper to taste

METHOD:
1. Cook leeks in salted water with rice. Allow to overcook. Drain. Place in food processor and purée. Season with salt and pepper. Set aside.
2. Fillet and wash the salmon-trout. Dry, and keep aside.
3. Butter the bottom of an oven-dish. Sprinkle with the finely chopped shallots. Place the seasoned fillets of salmon-trout in the dish. Top each of them with the leek mousse, and place 3 or 4 queen scallops on each. Pour the dry white wine around them.

4. Cook slowly in a pre-heated oven for 8 to 10 minutes, with a greased paper on top. When cooked, remove the salmon-trout: keep warm.
5. Strain the poaching stock into a shallow pan through a fine sieve. Reduce it by half. Add the Pernod and continue to reduce for another 2 to 3 minutes. Finally add the cream and cook for 3 to 4 minutes on a low heat.
6. Take the sauce off the heat and add the knob of cold butter, stir gently but thoroughly, while keeping warm. *Do not allow the sauce to reach boiling again!*
7. Place the trout fillets on individual plates or in a large dish. Pour the sauce over and garnish with pastry fleurons. Serve with boiled potatoes and fresh vegetables.

> ### HILTON-RICHFIELD
> *Fleurons make a professional-looking garnish for any dish. They are simply little figurines in all sorts of shapes, cut out of puff pastry. They can be little fishes for a fish dish, fruit-shapes for a dessert, or even straight geometrical diamonds, squares or oblongs. Use any left-over puff pastry for this. If you feel like making a lot, do so — they keep well in the deep-freezer and you can use them as required. Simply paint with egg yolk before baking for 5 minutes at 200°C.*

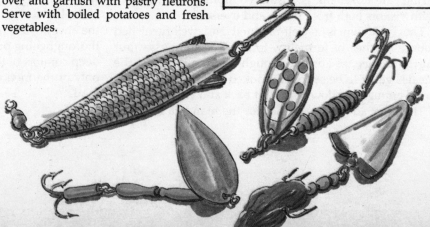

Méli-Mélo de Crustacés à l'Avocat et aux Oranges

INGREDIENTS:
4 small crayfish tails
8 queen prawns
8 medium langoustines
200 g peeled and deveined shrimps
8 crab legs, shelled
2 avocado pears, peeled and cut in
    halves, lengthwise
20 g pecan nuts, crushed
50 mℓ Van Der Hum liqueur
40 mℓ butter
few whole pecans nuts, for garnish
8 basil leaves, cut into fine strips
the zest of 2 oranges, all the pith
    removed, and the fruit segmented
50 mℓ Noilly Prat French vermouth
300 mℓ cream
salt and pepper to taste

METHOD:
1. Peel and devein all the shellfish if necessary. Boil the crab legs in salt water for 3 minutes before cracking the shells.
2. Place a sauté pan on the heat and add the butter. Sauté the assorted shellfish. Season this "salpicon" and keep it warm.
3. Deglaze the pan with Noilly Prat and Van Der Hum. Add the cream and cook slowly for 3 or 4 minutes, until lightly thickened.
4. Add the orange segments, crushed nuts and basil leaves. Season with salt and pepper and keep hot.
5. Cut the avocado into slices. Place the slices on one side of your serving plates, season with salt and pepper from a mill. Pour the méli-mélo on to the plates, garnish with whole pecan nuts and the orange zest, which must first be blanched by dropping into boiling water for 30 seconds, to remove any bitter taste. Serve with rice or boiled potatoes.

> ### HILTON-RICHFIELD
> *It seems to be a national custom to consider potatoes as an alternative to rice, and vice versa. If you have one, the feeling is, you don't serve the other. We can't see why not. A helping of well-seasoned, piquant rice on one side, and a plain boiled potato on the other, seems us to be a fine accompaniment to dishes such as this one.*
>
> *Most of us don't have much choice when it comes to buying potatoes. Cape readers are the lucky ones, for the potatoes there are the equal of any in the world. In other parts of the country, you have to take more or less whatever's available. Some spuds are fine for mashing and rotten for baking. Some are watery; some are starchy. There's very little consistency and, what's more, the average housewife doesn't even know what to look for. Overseas, women buy the type of potato they need for each particular purpose. But overseas is a long way away.*

Elangeni Hotel ★ ★ ★ ★ TYYY
63 Snell Parade, Durban 4001
Telephone: (031) 37-1321
PO Box 4094, Durban 4000
Closed Sunday and all lunchtimes
Fully licensed

Punchinello's

What a pleasant room this is! It covers a good deal of space, but the furnishing has been carried out so cunningly that you are not aware of it. As befits the principal dining-room of a large, four-star hotel, it is somewhat formal in concept: but, then, you see, it's also one of Durban's most popular resort hotels, so the atmosphere is relaxed, informal and thoroughly appreciated by its patrons.

Punchinello's sets out to be a speciality fish restaurant, and the menu-card reflects this policy. No matter what the condition of the market, despite seasonal difficulties in supply, this excellent room always has excellent crayfish, prawns, langoustines and other seafood on offer – at prices even the most niggardly cannot complain of.

(Of course, the card also provides non-fish eaters with anything they desire, but we're not too concerned with them in this particular book!)

The kitchen here is run completely separately from the rest of the hotel's food and beverage operation, and particularly from the extremely successful Japanese restaurant, the Sukihama, next door. Executive chef Erich Latzelsberger has a big hotel to run, but he takes particular pride in the continuing prosperity of Punchinello's.

A measure of its reputation is the number of local business-people who patronise this restaurant, while residents of the Elangeni and holidaymakers from other hotels in this resort city, are all to be seen at its tables.

Punchinello's success is a tribute to the food and beverage policy of Southern Sun Hotels, which encourages each hotel to develop its own philosophy and approach to the dining-room.

King Scallops "Pinocolada"

INGREDIENTS:
20 King scallops
3 eggs
400 ml shellfish bouillon (see
   "Standard Recipes")
60 ml Pinocolada
squeeze of lemon juice
100 g butter
200 g desiccated coconut
250 ml fresh cream
10 g fresh morels, sliced
parsley sprigs
seasoning to taste

METHOD:
1. Season the scallops with lemon juice and salt.
2. Beat the eggs and pour into a flat dish. Pour the desiccated coconut into another flat dish. Pass the scallops through the egg and then through the coconut, until well-covered.
3. Melt the butter in a pan and fry scallops slowly until cooked through.
4. In a saucepan, pour the shellfish bouillon and the fresh cream, and reduce over high heat by half.
5. Add the 15 ml of Pinocolada and the sliced morels. Add seasoning.

6. Cover the fried scallops with sauce and garnish with lemon wedges and parsley sprigs.

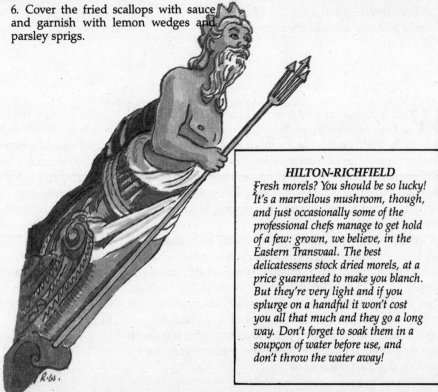

HILTON-RICHFIELD
Fresh morels? You should be so lucky! It's a marvellous mushroom, though, and just occasionally some of the professional chefs manage to get hold of a few: grown, we believe, in the Eastern Transvaal. The best delicatessens stock dried morels, at a price guaranteed to make you blanch. But they're very light and if you splurge on a handful it won't cost you all that much and they go a long way. Don't forget to soak them in a soupçon of water before use, and don't throw the water away!

Masala-Fried Chad with Tomato Chutney

INGREDIENTS:
8 cutlets of fresh chad (elf)
5 lemons
200 g onions, sliced
40 g garlic, pounded
10 g green chillies, pounded
½ bunch dhunia leaves (coriander)
60 g medium hot masala powder
250 mℓ oil
400 g tomatoes, blanched, peeled,
  chopped
20 g fresh ginger root
5 mℓ turmeric powder
salt

METHOD:
1. Pound together the ginger, garlic, chillies, with lemon juice and salt, to make a masala mixture.
2. Mix this mixture with the powdered masala and rub into the chad cutlets.
3. Heat the oil to medium temperature. Carefully place the fish cutlets in the oil (beware of spattering) and fry until cooked on both sides.
4. Make a tomato chutney: fry the onions in hot oil until brown. Add the turmeric, the remaining masala mixture, and the tomatoes. Add salt. Allow to simmer for 10 minutes. Garnish with fresh dhunia leaves (coriander).
5. Serve together with the fried chad cutlets.

HILTON-RICHFIELD
If you have a mortar and pestle, apothecary-style, it's worth-while making the effort to pound thin slices of fresh ginger with equally thin slices of the garlic. Add a little lemon juice to keep the mixture workable. This recipe calls for 5 lemons, but you may find this a bit much: the quantity can be reduced. Use some real Indian lemon pickle made by Pakco for that extra pizzazz. Chad, incidentally, is almost unknown away from the Natal coast, where it is caught year-round. In the Cape, it's known as elf, much sought-after during the summer. Musselcracker makes a perfect substitute. So does 74. NB. Johannesburg readers: before you get too frustrated, choose another recipe!

R. Ward '82

Valkenburg Manor,
off Liesbeek Avenue,
Observatory, Cape Town 7925
Telephone: (021) 47-6446
PO Box 2369, Cape Town 8000
Closed Mondays
Wine & Malt licence (pending)

Rosenfontein

Keith Blake and John Jackson are two men with stars in their eyes and the zeal of the true missionary. Their ambition is to have one of the finest restaurants in Cape Town, and one can only admire the determination and skill with which they have set about it.

Rosenfontein was a restaurant in Paarl that Blake and Jackson took over three years ago, with success. It was a tiny place, though, and chef Jackson and maître Blake honed their talents there, always with bigger things in view.

Valkenburg Manor House provided the bigger things. There, with artistic skill and businesslike fervour, a catering centre has been created, consisting of an up-market restaurant serving John Jackson's highly personalised version of French haute cuisine; a function room adjoining that can cater for 100; a lovely sheltered courtyard for salads and light luncheons; and the restored barn area

and garden surrounding it where homely, peasant-style food is served.

What a historical site! The land dates back to van Riebeeck and the architecture reflects the styles of the 18th century through to Victorian times. So precious is this heritage that the buildings and land belong to the National Monuments Council. The restorations cost a cool million and the Rosenfontein enterprise has a long lease.

John Jackson's cooking, as has been said, is not in the mainstream of modern French cuisine and it shows praiseworthy individuality. Particularly impressive, though, is his style of presentation. Every plate that comes from his kitchen is eye-catching and aesthetically pleasing. If, as they say, one eats first with the eyes, John's food will really hit the spot.

No doubt at all, Rosenfontein adds considerably to the gourmet amenities of the Fairest Cape.

Ceviche de Crevettes à l'Avocat, Sauce à la Crème d'Anis

(Marinated prawns with avocado and Pernod sauce)

20 good sized prawns raw, with or
  without heads
1 perfect, ripe avocado
THE CEVICHE MARINADE:
250 mℓ freshly squeezed lemon juice
1 clove garlic, minced
10 mℓ Pommery or other whole seed
  mustard
30 mℓ shredded fennel or dill leaves
2 or 3 fresh green herbs, for garnish
salt and pepper to taste

METHOD:
1. Make the ceviche marinade by mixing all the ingredients together. Note that the "cooking" process of the marinade will only work with fresh lemon juice. No success will be obtained with bottled, preserved juice.
2. Remove the heads and shells of the prawns, leaving only the tails attached. Cut each prawn in half along the spine, removing and discarding the intestine. Lay the prawn halves in the marinade for 3 to 4 hours until the flesh has become clear white, as when cooked in the normal manner. Drain well and reserve, keeping moist with a little of the mari-

nade. (After draining, you may wrap each prawn half tightly in plastic wrap, and they will hold well for several days.)

THE PERNOD SAUCE:
100 g cooked fennel bulb (cooked for
  half an hour in salted water)
10 mℓ whole seed mustard
75 mℓ olive oil
250 mℓ fresh cream
juice of 1 lemon
60 mℓ (or more) Pernod
a little milk
salt and pepper to taste

METHOD:
1. In a blender purée the cooked fennel bulb (it must be chilled) with the hard-boiled egg yolks, the mustard and lemon juice. Dribble in the olive oil slowly. Remove to a mixing bowl.
2. In the mixing bowl blend in the cream and Pernod. Adjust for seasoning. If the sauce is too thick a good pouring consistency may be obtained by adding a little milk. Chill until required.

SERVING
1. Pour a pool of the sauce on to each

serving place. Arrange a fan of five prawns on the perimeter at the top of the plate, with the tails outermost.
2. Cut the avocado into quarters, removing the skin. Keeping each quarter intact, cut them into 2 mm thick slices to a distance of 2 cm from the apex of the quarters. With the fingers, gently fan out the avocado and lay on the serving plates opposite the fan of prawns, with the uncut apex at the centre of each plate. Garnish with delicate, green, fresh herbs.

HILTON-RICHFIELD
There are hundreds of variations of the "ceviche" in Latin-America, where this method originated (Peru, actually, although today it is served in many countries, including those of Europe). The Japanese are not the only people who enjoy their fish raw (sashimi); in South America they actually eat prawns and such-like without even marinating them! And there are some folk in odd parts of the world who think we are quite crazy to eat oysters raw! One man's meat is another man's poisson!

196

Graça was the vino.

There are many ways of enjoying Graça.
But here's a simple recipe that seems to work every time.
First, take a tableful of friendino's of assorted sexes, as shown. Place in a warm, cheerful and not too sedate ambience.
Mix in the speciality of the house. In this case, prawns with lemon butter.
And throughout, marinade generously with the most important ingredient of all.
Graça.
A crisp, earthy white wine.
With a very slight sparkle.
A decidedly different taste.
And an unusual effect on what happens around it.

Graça.
The talking,
eating, drinking,
laughing, singing,
sharing wine.

Produced in the Republic of South Africa.

Les Crevettes Rôties, Beurre Blanc et Beurre Rose

(Roasted or pan-fried prawns with white and pink butter sauces)

24 good-size prawns, with or without
    heads, raw
rice to your own recipe
FOR THE BEURRE BLANC:
75 mℓ dry white wine
10 mℓ chives, chopped coarsely
25 mℓ fresh cream
45 mℓ cider vinegar
90 g butter, chilled
a little arrowroot (cornflour will do)
FOR THE BEURRE ROSE
75 mℓ dry red wine
30 mℓ fresh lemon juice
10 mℓ chives, coarsely chopped
30 mℓ fresh cream
90 g butter, chilled
a little arrowroot (cornflour will do)

METHOD:
1. Prepare the raw prawns by cutting the heads off (reserve them for other uses). Remove the shells except for the last segment and the tail itself. Remove the alimentary tube. Chill.
2. If rice is being served as an accompaniment, cook it now.

BEURRE BLANC:
3. In a small saucepan, put the white wine, vinegar and chives, and reduce over high heat until only an essence remains coating the bottom of the pan. Remove from the heat and add cream. Add just enough arrowroot (or cornflour), dissolved in a little cold water and smoothed, to thicken the mixture just slightly: this will stabilise the sauce. Season to taste. Over low heat, whisk in the cold butter. Reserve over low heat.

BEURRE ROSE:
4. In a small saucepan put the red wine, vinegar and chives, and reduce until only an essence remains coating the bottom of the pan. Remove from the heat. Add the cream and lemon juice. Add just enough arrowroot (or cornflour) to thicken the mixture slightly. Season to taste and over low heat whisk in the cold butter. Reserve until required.

NOTE:
Take care not to let either sauce come to the boil again, or the butter will separate. If the sauce does cool too much it can be heated again gently to just below boiling point. Stir the sauces every few minutes until required.

5. About five minutes before serving, heat a frying-pan large enough to accommodate all the prawns at once. Add enough butter to coat the bottom liberally. As the butter browns, add the prawns, seasoning to taste. If desired some chopped fresh herbs and garlic may be added at this point for a more robust flavour (though this may overwhelm the delicate sauces). Cook the prawns for a minute or two on each side, before moving them to a hot oven to roast until cooked through.
6. Bring the sauces to serving temperature. Press the rice into small timbales and empty one on each plate, at the edge. Pouring one sauce at a time, cover half the plate with each sauce, the dividing line corresponding with the centre of each timbale of rice.
7. Arrange 6 prawns in a crescent around the rice, three on each sauce, with the tails pointing to the outside of the plates. Garnish with bright green fresh herbs. Serve immediately.
NOTE: It is important to work very quickly from the moment the sauces are poured on to the plates, so that they do not deteriorate before the guest is served.

HILTON-RICHFIELD

A delightful dish that depends for its effect as much on presentation as it does on cooking. It shows, we think, the influence of the great chef Roger Vergé at whose marvellous restaurant "Le Moulin de Mougins" in the south of France chef John Jackson studied for a short time. We like his note at the end of this recipe. One of the marks of the good cook, as against the just competent cook, is the ability to work fast. That depends usually on two things: practice, and the "mise-en-place" – having everything you're going to need ready for use, all prepared and rarin' to go. In other words, good organisation.

Royal Hotel ★ ★ ★ ★ TYYY
267 Smith Street, Durban 4001
Telephone: (031) 304-0331
PO Box 1041, Durban 4000
Closed Saturday lunch, Sunday evening
Fully licensed

Royal Grill

*T*he Royal has been a Durban landmark for many years. Before it was extended outwards and upwards, it had rather an air of old colonial Natal – not quite last century, but certainly pre-war (take your pick as to which one).

The Royal Grill was always among the best restaurants in the city, and it still is. The modernisation all around it has affected the Grill only in terms of the efficiency of the kitchen. The quality of the food, the absolutely impeccable service by the finest brigade of waiting personnel in the country, the magnificence of the tables and their accoutrements, even the discreet tinkle of music in the background (where it belongs), remain as always.

The niceties of high-class service are properly observed here. Food is served from the correct side, your wine is poured with the respect it deserves, everything runs smoothly and discreetly.

Menu and cooking live up to the standards the room demands. You would be wrong to expect flights of culinary fancy in an international à la carte restaurant such as this. Here, the standard and classical dishes of France and the West are given expert treatment by as expert a group of chefs as you could wish to meet. That should not stop you asking for something special, something not on the menu: everyone will certainly do what they can to please.

Then, suddenly, you happen on the Royal Grill one Sunday lunchtime, and a dramatic change is evident. What used to be sleepy Sundays for The Royal Grill have been transformed into frenzied activity.

For on Sunday the Grill presents a buffet – large, lavish and luxuriant, and at a low price that must surely represent the best value for money in all Africa. It's truly astonishing, and Durban has been quick to send her hordes here for a jolly good Sunday feed-up. Same ambience, same tables, same luxury, but at prices affordable for every ordinary citizen in the town.

Escalopes of Kingklip

INGREDIENTS:
4 x 150 g fillets of kingklip
250 mℓ salmon mousseline (see recipe below)
1 shallot or onion, finely chopped
juice of ½ lemon
150 g cold butter
Chinese sesame seed oil
50 mℓ Noilly Prat vermouth
1 ℓ fish stock (see "Standard Recipes")
250 mℓ dry white wine
250 mℓ cream
250 g julienned carrots, leeks and celery

THE SALMON MOUSSELINE:
350 g fresh salmon
125 mℓ fresh cream
pinch cayenne pepper
2 egg whites
salt and pepper to taste
All the above must be very cold before working with it.
8 prawns, cooked, shelled down to the tail only (for garnish)

METHOD:
1. Prepare the salmon mousseline by putting the salmon through a blender or processor. Remove to a bowl and whisk in the cream, followed by the egg whites. Keep cold.
2. Ask your fishmonger to give you fairly thick fillets of kingklip. Trim them, removing the excess white that sometimes appears on the back.
3. With a very sharp knife, carefully slit open the fillets from the right-hand side towards the left, taking care not to reach the left-hand edge. This gives you a kind of envelope. Lightly season inside and out with salt, cayenne and lemon juice.
4. Spoon the mousseline into a plastic bag, of which one very small corner has been cut off. Pipe the mousseline on to the bottom of each fillet, then close the fillet by folding over the top half. (Before closing, dribble in a few drops of Chinese sesame oil: it imparts a slight but delicious flavour.)
5. Place the filled fillets in a pan, and under the right-hand side of each slip a piece of buttered greaseproof paper, folded over to cover the opening. Put in the fish stock, white wine and Noilly Prat, season with salt, pepper and lemon juice. Poach for a few minutes but do not allow to overcook.
6. Remove the fillets and keep warm. Reduce the stock by two-thirds. Add the cream and the julienne of vegetables. Reduce by half, and finish with the very cold butter, whisking it in. Correct seasoning and consistency.
7. Coat the kingklip with the sauce, making sure each spoonful contains some of the vegetable julienne. Place two prawns on each fillet, the tails (still in their shells) towards the middle.

HILTON-RICHFIELD
Hooray — now we've found another use for those unwanted plastic bags! After you've mucked it up with mousseline and cut off the corner, though, there's nothing for it but to chuck it away. These remarks, of course, do not apply to superior home-cooks who are fully equipped with a pair of piping-bags and a set of all the little doo-dahs you squeeze through.

Fillet of Trout "Simplon"

INGREDIENTS:

8 x 300g trout, skinned and filleted
150 g cooked shrimps, chopped
400 g white mushrooms, finely diced
5 tomatoes, blanched, skinned, seeded and chopped coarsely (tomato concassé)
1 *l* crayfish sauce (see "Standard Recipes")
50 g butter
8 mussels in shell, for garnish
1 onion or shallot, finely chopped
1 English cucumber, finely diced
pinch each dried marjoram, thyme and cayenne pepper
8 slices tomato, for garnish
salt and pepper to taste

METHOD:

1. Slightly flatten each trout fillet and clip the side skin with a pair of kitchen scissors or a very sharp knife, to even the edges.

2. Melt the butter in a pan and cook the onion or shallot, without allowing it to colour. Now add the mushrooms. Cook together until dry (this makes a "duxelles"). The mixture can be dried further in a strainer, using the back of a spoon to press it.

3. Season to taste. Return to a pan, add the shrimps, cucumber and tomato concassé. Lightly flavour with herbs and cayenne. Simmer for a few minutes, then leave to cool.

4. Lay a trout fillet skin-side down (it has already been skinned), spoon the duxelles mixture on to it, place another fillet on top, skin side up, thus forming a sandwich. Two fillets with one filling is a portion.

5. Wrap in aluminium foil, make the package airtight, and cook in a steamer, or in a colander over boiling water, for approx. 5 minutes.

6. Remove from foil, drain and discard the juice (unless you have another use for it), and place the fish on an oval hot plate. Coat with prepared crayfish sauce. Decorate with slices of fresh tomato and the mussels in their shells.

HILTON-RICHFIELD

This is a fine, sophisticated recipe, typical of the excellent cooking at the Royal Grill. We must admit, though, that the best trout we've ever eaten have been those we've just taken out of the river, cleaned, and chucked in a pan of butter over a fire we've built ourselves — eaten not ten minutes after leaving the water! (Who needs cook-books?)

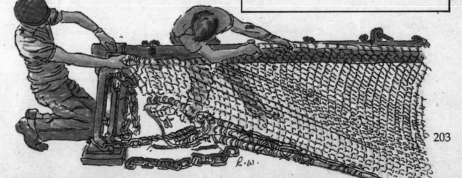

Sun City Hotel,
Sun City, Pilanesberg,
Bophuthatswana
Telephone: (014651) 21000
PO Box 1, Sun City
Closed lunchtimes
Fully licensed

Silver Forest

*S*pend a day at incredible Sun City, and when you get hungry you can have a hot dog or a hamburger or a pie at the fast food facility out on the Terrace, or a quick (and beautifully prepared) lunch in the Calabash, the Sun City Hotel's all-day room. It'll all be good and pleasant, but nothing will have prepared you for the sheer excellence of the Silver Forest restaurant, which opens only for dinner.

This is a room up to any international standard you care to name. Recently the management made minor adjustments to the décor, to give the room a feeling of greater space. One of these days, perhaps, they might find a suitable alternative to those dead wooden twigs with little white lights up and down them, which give the room its name.

Apart from that the room is luxurious in its comfort, and the setting of the tables with its crisp linen, sparkling crystal and heavy cutlery, tells you immediately that you are in a restaurant of high quality. The menu is astonishingly varied, considering the distance the complex is from all sources of supply (except for its meat, which comes from Mafikeng nearby, and which has become a by-word for excellence).

The card is clearly written, simply stated and without hype or purple prose. And the cooking reaches standards of brilliance at times that would do justice to a Michelin-starred establishment in France.

The appointments, the décor, the service give an impression of formality, of course: a dinner-only dining-room has to conform to the conventions of the night. This is a resort, though, after all, and dress here can be very loose and informal.

Relax and enjoy it, and look northwards in the knowledge that there's no better food anywhere in Africa between here and Cairo.

Fishpörkolt

This is a traditional Hungarian dish. It can be made from various kinds of fish, such as kingklip, butterfish, yellowtail, barracuda, 74, merlu, red roman and others.

INGREDIENTS:
(serves 6)
1,2 kg fillets of fish cut into 2 cm cubes
80 g butter
30 g fresh garlic, chopped
50 mℓ tomato paste
1 ℓ water
4 bay leaves
250 mℓ sour cream
2 medium onions
3 green peppers, deseeded, cut into
  2 cm squares
250 mℓ dry white wine
100 mℓ paprika
600 g potatoes, peeled, cut into cubes
salt, white pepper to taste

METHOD:
1. Fry the onions in butter until brown in colour, add garlic, green peppers and tomato paste.
2. Stir in the paprika, then add the white wine and water.
3. Add salt and white pepper to taste, and the bay leaves. Bring to the boil and allow to simmer for about 15 minutes.
4. Add the potatoes and, 20 minutes later, add the fish.
5. Simmer for a further 10 to 15 minutes and then add more salt and pepper, if necessary. If the sauce is weak, thicken it with cornflour or arrowroot, softened in a little water.
6. Before serving add the sour cream, but do not boil the pörkolt any more. Serve with a fresh green salad.

HILTON-RICHFIELD
Most of the paprika sold here under brand-names is, regrettably, of dreadful quality. It only has the colour but hardly a trace of the real taste, and certainly very little strength. It's often used by bad cooks simply to add colour. If you can't get any of the genuine Hungarian article, and you have to use the local stuff, add a little cayenne pepper to give it something like the proper Magyar zing.

Graça with friendino's.

There are many ways to enjoy crisp white Graça.
With a handful of sardino's.
Or a lorryload of langoustino's.
The most rewarding way, however, is with a tableful of friendino's.
That way you get to share not just a refreshing taste, but also a sparkling experience.

**Graça.
The talking,
eating, drinking,
laughing, singing,
sharing wine.**

Produced in the Republic of South Africa.

Gefilte Fish

This is a traditional Jewish dish with its origin in Poland. It is served mostly on Friday evening when the "Shabbath" is welcomed, and on other festive occasions. Gefilte Fish is garnished with carrot slices and hard-boiled eggs, and is served with hot, horseradish sauce ("chraine") and fish jelly. The authentic fish to use for this dish is carp.

INGREDIENTS:
1,5 kg to 1,8 kg fresh carp
FOR THE FISH JELLY:
1 kg fish bones and skin
2 carrots
10 mℓ dried thyme, or 30 g fresh thyme
1 ℓ water
2 onions, sliced
50 g (2 sticks) celery, with stalks and leaves
20 mℓ dried fennel, or 50 g fresh fennel
5 mℓ gelatine (soaked in water)
salt and white pepper to taste
FOR THE FISH DUMPLINGS:
the filleted carp (you should have about 500 g)
150 g onion
2 carrots
3 ℓ water

250 g white bread
80 g (½ bunch) parsley
4 eggs
salt, white pepper, sugar
FOR THE HORSERADISH SAUCE:
80 g creamed horseradish
squeeze of lemon juice
200 g beetroot, boiled, peeled (if in a hurry, use a can, drained)
sugar
FOR THE GARNISH:
2 hard-boiled eggs, sliced
2 carrots, sliced

METHOD:
1. Cut fish into fillets and remove skin.

FISH JELLY:
2. Cook fish bones, head and skin in 1 ℓ water with onion, carrots, celery, thyme, bay leaves and fennel. Bring to the boil and simmer for 30 minutes.
3. Remove the foam from the top with a spoon.
4. Strain and reserve the stock. Spice the stock with salt, white pepper and lemon juice.
5. Add soaked gelatine to the stock. Stir well and put it in a cold place. (Fish Stock no. 1)

FISH STOCK:
Take the solid remnants from the fish jelly stock (step 4 above), add 3 ℓ water and 15 mℓ salt to them. Bring to the boil and simmer. (Fish Stock No. 2)

FISH DUMPLINGS:
1. Mince the carp fillets together with the white bread, onions and parsley. (A processor will do this very fast.)
2. Mix slightly and add 4 eggs. Season with salt, sugar and white pepper. (A pinch of sugar only.)
3. If the mixture is too weak, add more white bread.
4. From this fish mixture, form dumplings (about 50 g each, the size of a large egg). Put them gently into Fish Stock no. 2 and let them simmer for about 15 minutes.
5. Remove the dumplings and keep them in a cool place.

HORSERADISH SAUCE:
Mix the creamed horseradish and the grated beetroot, season with salt, sugar and lemon juice.

Garnish the fish dumplings with hard-boiled eggs, sliced, and carrot slices; serve with the fish jelly. The horseradish sauce should be served separately.

HILTON-RICHFIELD

This is probably the most delicious and the best-known of all traditional Jewish dishes. It can be made with a mixture of hard and soft-fleshed fish (a little game fish, some yellowtail, some hake, etc) but carp is the best. Recently, dam-bred carp has been appearing on the fish counters of some of our supermarkets. Checkers in the Transvaal certainly has it. It isn't as muddy as the wild carp and can be used straight off the counters, without pre-soaking in fresh water.

31 Aliwal Street,
Durban 4001
Telephone: (031) 304-2018
PO Box 10927, Marine Parade 4056
Closed Saturday lunch and Sundays
Fully licensed

St Géran

Some years ago, during a general exodus of French citizens from Mauritius to South Africa, many worthy souls floundered a little, not knowing how to go about earning a living.

In many cases, the new immigrants turned to food. They believed, as so many disillusioned newcomers believed, that anyone could open and run a restaurant, and make a good thing out of it. Most of them failed.

The Mauvis family was an exception. They came to Durban from Mauritius, but they were already professionals, steeped in the European tradition of the family restaurant. St Géran was a hit from Day One, and that was a long time ago.

Robert Mauvis still runs the room, while his mother and his brother look after the kitchens. The standard of service here is excellent, and the Mauritian dishes the Mauvis family conjure up bring a touch of the spices of the Indian Ocean to Durban's generally conservative tastes.

The cooking of Mauritius is quite fascinating. it's an amalgam of the provincial food of France "metropolitaine", the herbs and spices of India, the subtleties and contrasts of Chinese cooking as adapted by the many Far Eastern immigrants to Mauritius, and a "je ne sais quoi" of mystery — attributable to the French influence — which has become known as "cuisine créole". It's a hearty, strong, clearly-stated philosophy of food that is wide enough to form the basis of a speciality menu.

And here at St Géran, the philosophy is realised beautifully. If your palate enjoys chillies, here they are: very light if that's your taste, very heavy if you like to sweat while you eat! Just ask! But that's the crude side of Mauritian cookery. Its blend of spices, particularly with seafood, is far more subtle and sophisticated than the heartstopping heat of chilli!

Of course, the restaurant offers a whole range of dishes, too, that are classical French — not heavily spiced and acceptable to even the least adventurous of palates. They're also a part of créole cuisine.

Crab St Géran

(A hot starter)

INGREDIENTS:
2 large fresh crabs
100 g butter
2 spring onion, finely chopped
100 mℓ milk
1 medium onion, finely chopped
100 g margarine
100 g grated Gruyère or Emmenthaler cheese
white sauce

METHOD:
1. Place crabs in large pot in cold water that comes half-way up the depth of the shells. Bring to the boil and continue boiling for 10 minutes.
2. Remove crab and break off the legs. Remove the top flat section of the shell and with a fine fork or your fingers remove all the flesh. Break the legs and winkle out the flesh. Be careful to get rid of all tiny fragments of broken shell, which are sometimes difficult to see. (The water you have boiled the crab in could, if you wished, be boiled rapidly and reduced very drastically; cooled, poured into a bakkie or bag, and frozen for another use.)
3. Melt margarine in a pan, place onions in it and cook slowly until soft. Do not allow to colour.
4. Add the butter, melt it, then add the spring onions. Simmer for 2 minutes.
5. Add the crab meat to the onion mixture, then add the milk. Simmer for 4 minutes.
6. Remove from heat, but do not let it get too cool. In the meantime, heat up the white sauce in a small pot and when hot remove from heat, and add the grated cheese. Allow to dissolve in the sauce while off the stove.
7. Now add the white sauce and cheese to the crab mixture, heat gently to serving temperature, and serve in the flat crab shells, which will have been cleaned for this purpose, or in scallop shells.

HILTON-RICHFIELD
A most original recipe for fresh crab. For those of us away from the coast it's probably only of academic interest: how often do you see fresh crabs in your part of the world? The days when they used to come in three times a week from Lourenço Marques are long gone. We do not recommend the frozen Alaska crab in the supermarkets. Frozen crab loses most of its taste and also some of its consistency. It just isn't worth the money.

Fish Vindaye

INGREDIENTS:
1,5 kg barracuda or yellowtail, headless, gutted, sliced
15 mℓ garlic, crushed
500 mℓ cooking oil
5 mℓ fresh ginger root, crushed
8 whole fresh hot chillies
15 mℓ salt
30 mℓ turmeric
100 mℓ white vinegar
800 g pickling onions, chopped
pinch black peppercorns, crushed

METHOD:
1. Mix turmeric and vinegar in a bowl.
2. Fry sliced fish in a pan in oil, sprinkle lightly with salt and crushed black peppercorns. When cooked, remove all skin and bones, leaving chunks of cooked fish.
3. In a separate pot pour remaining oil, add onions, chillies, little salt. Simmer slowly until onions and chillies are cooked through. Add garlic, ginger, and simmer for 2 minutes. Then add mixture of turmeric and vinegar and simmer for a further 2 minutes.
4. Switch off heat, then add the fish. Mix well. Check for seasoning, and serve.

HILTON-RICHFIELD

Mauritian cookery is fascinating. It combines Indian, Chinese, Arabic and traces of African with traditional French culinary values, and becomes something unique. "Créole" is the term for it, but Mauritian créole is quite distinct from the créole dishes of, say, New Orleans or Martinique, or even French West Africa (that was). Funny thing about Mauritian cooking: the closer to sea level, the fiercer and more pungent it is, while the higher up the mountain you go, where property is more expensive, the closer the cooking becomes to France itself.

This vindaye, incidentally, should be kept at room temperature for 24 hours. After that, you can safely keep it in the fridge for days.

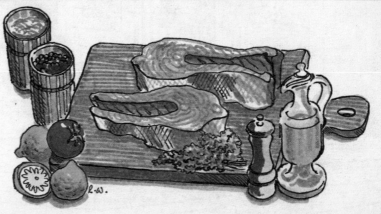

Johannesburg Sun & Towers ★ ★ ★ ★ ★ TYYY
84 Smal Street, Johannesburg Central
Telephone: (011) 29-7011
PO Box 535, Johannesburg 2000
Closed Saturday lunch and Sundays
Fully licensed

St James

The newest-comer to the scene of Grand Dining-Out in central Johannesburg, the St James, represents all that is best in a five-star hotel's international grillroom and restaurant.

Big tables, set far apart from each other; marble floors and columns; a high ceiling; service from the most efficient brigade in the country; a young French chef who spent several months in the kitchens of the great Paul Bocuse in Lyon, France. Sit here, close your eyes and think of – well, any grand five-star dining room in any capital city of the world.

And it's a clever menu they offer you here. Different enough from the usual run of hotel grill-rooms to be interesting, but not so outlandish that the diner recoils from the card and orders a steak in self-defence, the St James combines dignity with a modern outlook on the culinary arts that really works.

Under the supervision of executive chef Brian McCune and the more distant but nonetheless deeply concerned eye of the great Billy Gallagher, the dishes offered are sized somewhere between the contemptuous pinprick offerings of "nouvelle cuisine" and the overheaped plates of hot dinner so beloved of too many South Africans. This is an international room, after all, and it has become extremely successful in its very short life. One of its attractions is a range of French wines chosen, bottled and labelled by the great Bocuse himself.

You will not expect to pay snack bar-prices here, but neither need you fear an inflated bill, unrepresentative of what you have eaten. Visitors from overseas, of course, cannot believe the low prices: low not only because of the rate of exchange, but by comparison with the prices in other restaurants all over the world. South Africa must surely be the gastronomical bargain-hunter's paradise!

And because of the comforting reasonableness of the bill, this restaurant has become the favourite room for formal parties, for celebrations, for that intimate night out you have been promising yourself for so long.

215

Monkfish Curry with Fresh Fruit

INGREDIENTS:
**1 kg monkfish fillets cut into large
  dice, and dredged in flour**
4 cloves fresh ginger, finely crushed
10 m*l* good quality curry powder
75 g butter
**250 m*l* fish stock (see "Standard
  Recipes")**
1 small onion, finely diced
salt and white pepper to taste
THE SAUCE:
100 m*l* dry white wine
squeeze of lemon juice
250 m*l* cream
25 g cold butter, to finish sauce
THE GARNISH:
**Fresh sliced fruit in season: peaches,
  nectarines, plums, pineapple, apple,
  etc.**

METHOD:
1. Place white wine and fish stock in saucepan over high heat and reduce by two-thirds.
2. Add cream and simmer for 5 minutes.
3. Sauté the onion, ginger and curry powder in the butter, to allow the curry to release its flavour.
4. Add diced monkfish to the curry and cook through.
5. Just before serving, whisk 25 g cold butter into the white wine, fish stock and cream sauce, to thicken it. Finally, add a squeeze of lemon to sharpen the flavour.
6. Pour the sauce into the pan with the monkfish, and combine gently.
7. Serve with saffron rice and garnish with slices of whatever fresh fruit in available.
(If you use apples or pears, be sure to sprinkle with lemon juice to stop them discolouring.)

Master-Chef Brian McCune says: Curry powder is a western, and specifically British, invention. It is certainly never used in India! If you have an Indian market near you, why not experiment a little? For flavour, use ginger, cumin and coriander. For hotness, chilli; for aroma use cardamon, fennel and star aniseed; put in some turmeric for colour and cinnamon or cassia for a little sweetness.

HILTON-RICHFIELD
See the section on spices in the Introduction for some useful tips on how to keep them. If you must have some handy, though, and you prefer to grind your own rather than use the commercial varieties, remember they have a very limited shelf life. Grind only a little of each at a time, and keep them in some of those plastic medicine containers whose contents you stopped using ages ago. The rest, no matter how they are packed, should go into the coldest part of your deep-freezer. They'll keep for a long, long time.

Monkfish, by the way, is sometimes substituted for crayfish in unscrupulous restaurants, especially in seafood cocktails. With pink gunge covering it, it could pass!

Seafood Strudel with Sweet Pepper Sauce

INGREDIENTS:
**800 g diced seafood, including
kingklip, linefish, shrimps, mussels
500 mℓ cream
small bunch of fresh dill or chervil
(chopped)
100 g butter
250 mℓ white wine
200 g phyllo pastry, from a Greek
delicatessen
salt and white pepper**
THE SAUCE:
**3½ large red peppers, peeled,
deseeded, diced (the remaining
½pepper julienned for garnish)
½ onion, diced
500 mℓ cream
50 g butter
paprika
salt and white pepper**

METHOD:
1. Sauté the diced seafood in butter until just firm. Remove from pan and allow to cool.
2. Add white wine to pan and reduce by two-thirds. Add cream and reduce again to a coating consistency.
3. Add seasoning and chopped dill or chervil.
4. Mix the seafood into the sauce and allow to cool, but not to get cold.
5. Working quickly with the phyllo pastry (it dries very fast) lay out a large square of about 3 to 4 thicknesses. Brush with melted butter. Spread the seafood mixture over it and roll up like a Swiss roll, tucking in the ends. Brush again with melted butter and place on a greased baking tray. Bake at about 200°C for 10 to 12 minutes. Check frequently, as this is very fragile pastry.

THE SAUCE:
6. Meanwhile, sauté the diced peppers with the diced onion in butter.
7. Put the mixture in the blender with the cream, and process.
8. Return the mixture to the pan and correct seasoning with paprika, salt and pepper. Reduce a little and add the remaining ½ pepper, sliced to a very fine julienne.
9. Carefully cut the strudel in slices and serve with the sauce and a separate green salad.

HILTON-RICHFIELD
It's advisable to paint each single square of phyllo pastry with melted butter right through this recipe. A method for peeling peppers is given at the end of "Standard Recipes".

217

Civic Theatre, Braamfontein
Johannesburg 2001
Telephone: (011) 30-2933
PO Box 31246, Braamfontein 2017
Closed Saturday lunch and Sundays
Fully licensed

Symposium

A pleasant restaurant on the first floor of the Johannesburg Civic Theatre, the Symposium would be no more than that were it not for two factors. One is the availability here of beautifully fresh produce that's often hard to find anywhere else, and the other is the personality of the owner, Dimitri Hadjeandreou.

Dimitri (no one bothers with that difficult surname!) has always been here, it seems, and he is one of the most interesting characters in the entire restaurant business. A Greek from Alexandria (where all the best Greeks come from, the Alexandrian Greeks will tell you), Dimitri has a warmth and charm that convince you they are genuine — and they are, for he really enjoys people — and a kind of schizophrenic ability to divide himself between his smoothly-run dining-room and his equally efficient kitchen.

The day's offerings are brought to your tableside for approval. Steaks, trimmed and cut to perfection: lamb cutlets; the tiny fillet of a milk-fed calf; properly sized tournedos; a skewer of four cuts from a saddle of lamb; a big platter of fish, dressed and filleted, including sometimes a rare 74, a mussel-cracker and of course the ubiquitous kingklip; plates of fresh oysters and mussels, and some made up with unusual Greek speciality salads and other starters. All are prepared an hour before the service starts, and all are immensely attractive and tempting.

If the time is convenient, though, and if Alexandrian-Greek food is to your taste, Dimitri will disappear into his kitchen and emerge triumphantly with a meal of Greek-style dishes that you will remember for a long, long time. He is the finest specialist in Eastern Mediterranean dishes we have encountered.

When there's a popular show on at the Civic Theatre, early dinner can be a bit of a rush, but you will get to your seat in time. Best to come when the patrons have gone in, though, and enjoy your meal at leisure.

Athinaiki Mayioneza

(Fish Athenian Style)

INGREDIENTS:
1 kg fish (any firm, white fish, such as rock cod, steenbras, or even fresh kingklip)
1,5 ℓ court-bouillon (see "Standard Recipes")
olives
beetroots
capers
pickled cucumber
boiled potatoes
carrots
gherkins
walnuts
boiled eggs
home-made mayonnaise
any other garnish items you like
salt and pepper to taste

METHOD:
1. Cook the fish whole, briefly, in the court-bouillon. Remove, skin and bone it carefully. The flesh is broken by hand ("let your fingers do the walking through the bony places") into small portions.
2. Boil some good quality potatoes and carrots. Skin the potatoes and cut into chunks; same with the carrots.
3. Mix together with the pieces of fish, and reassemble it all on a long platter, in a mound.
4. Cover the mound with home-made mayonnaise, which should be more lemoney and garlickey than the store-bought variety.
5. Now exercise your imagination in decorating the platter with colours and patterns, using boiled shaped beetroot pieces, capers and gherkins, boiled eggs, black olives, etc.

You can display the platter as a centrepiece at a buffet party, or serve it in individual portions as a first course. Ideally, a bottle of good, Greek retsina wine goes with this dish, but of course any good, strong-tasting wine of the Cape (not a sweet one) suits it.

HILTON-RICHFIELD
This recipe gives only a small idea of the ebullient personality and the fine culinary skills of Dimitri (or would you rather practise saying "Mr Hadjiandreou"?). Although the Symposium restaurant serves mainly western dishes, to the admiring approval of its many customers, give Dimitri an opportunity of creating an Eastern Mediterranean meal for you. It's a superb gastronomic experience.

Fish-Kebab With Prunes

Can be made with rock cod, musselcracker, kingklip, red roman or any firm, white fish.

INGREDIENTS:
600 g skinned linefish
24 stoneless prunes
30 mℓ ouzo
a little olive oil
150 g prosciutto ham (see note)
60 mℓ brandy
crayfish sauce (see "Standard
    Recipes") or sauce Choron (see note
    below)
salt and pepper to taste

METHOD:
1. Soak the prunes in brandy for 2 hours.
2. Cut the fish into small cubes, and soak them in ouzo for about 2 hours.
3. On 8 skewers, two per guest, place first a piece of fish, then a prune, then a piece of raw smoked ham. Season with salt and pepper. Drip on the olive oil. Cook under a grill or a broiler, turning carefully.
4. Spread some crayfish sauce or sauce Choron over your serving plates, and lay the cooked skewers on top.

HILTON-RICHFIELD

Ouzo is the first choice to marinate the fish in, but of course French Pernod will do, or even Ricard. If you don't use ouzo, don't dare call the dish Greek! Try to use a good Greek olive oil, though: it has a certain quality no other oil attains. For this dish you can use any raw ham: Italian prosciutto, such as Parma ham, French Bayonne, German Westphalian, Spanish serrano, or any ham of this type made by a top speciality meat firm, such as the splendid Taurus in Johannesburg or Rietmanns in Cape Town. Sauce Choron, by the way, is simply a Hollandaise with the addition of some chopped ripe tomato, skinned and seeded, a spoonful of tomato paste, warmed in a saucepan.

The Carlton ★★★★★ TYYY
Carlton Centre, Commissioner Street,
Johannesburg 2001
Telephone: (011) 331-8911
PO Box 7709, Johannesburg 2000
Closed Sunday lunch and Mondays
Fully licensed

The Three Ships

*F*or 15 years now The Three Ships has been purveying French-style "haute cuisine" to connoisseurs of good food, both local and from overseas. During this time, the management has seen many changes in the tastes of Johannesburg diners. When The Carlton opened there were pitifully few central Johannesburg restaurants offering really good food. Due to some extent to the example set by The Three Ships, both public taste and the trade's willingness to cater to it have been up-graded.

The room, of course, is the epitome of grace and elegance. Utterly luxurious, with only the finest linen, crystal and silver, it is serviced by as smooth a brigade of waiters as one could wish to meet.

One of the tricky techniques of the waiting profession is not to be noticed until you are wanted. The brigade here melts into the carpeting and the décor so unobtrusively that, when you do notice them, you are surprised to see how young they all are. Men who have trained here are now in top positions all over the country.

The food cannot be bettered. It is still "haute cuisine française" and it is in the hands of a talented young Englishman, Glynn Sinclair, whose hobby is entering professional chefs' competitions – and winning them all. He must be the most decorated chef in South Africa by now! The executive sous-chef of The Carlton is another Englishman, Stephen Pidgeley, and he is just as brilliant, though perhaps too busy to go in for all that competitive cookery. Both have contributed recipes to this book.

When we tell you that they have simplified their recipes somewhat for use by home cooks, you will begin to understand the meticulous and intricate preparation that goes on in a kitchen as high-class as that of The Three Ships.

Le Panache de Six Poissons "Christiane"
(by Chef Stephen Pidgeley)

INGREDIENTS:

2 medium crayfish tails
4 large scallops, or 8 small
4 x 40 g kingklip, filleted
4 medium king prawns, deveined
4 x 40 g linefish, filleted
1 medium trout
100 mℓ sparkling wine
150 mℓ fresh cream
3 mℓ saffron threads
**1 ripe tomato, blanched, peeled,
    deseeded**
**200 mℓ fish stock (see "Standard
    Recipes")**
25 g butter
20 g carrot
20 g celery   all julienned
20 g leek
15 g extra butter
freshly ground pepper

METHOD:

1. Cut the two crayfish tails straight down the centre with a medium length strong knife.
2. Wash the prawns and with a small strong knife cut a shallow incision down the back of each, just enough to clean out the alimentary tube inside.
3. Remove the head and tail from the trout. Wash and dry the fish, then cut across into four equal pieces, still on the bone.
4. Cut the kingklip and linefish fillets into two different shapes (for presentation purposes only).
5. Season the crayfish, prawns and trout.
6. Place the crayfish, prawns and trout in a shallow pan (*sauteuse*) with the wine and half the fish stock. Cover with a piece of buttered paper and bring to the boil on the stove.
7. Preheat oven to 180°C. When the pan is steaming (do not let it boil) place it in the oven and cook for 1½ minutes.
8. Remove from the oven, add the remaining fish (the kingklip and linefish) and poach for 2 more minutes.
9. When all the fish is cooked, take out of the pan and arrange on a platter. Sprinkle well with some fish stock and keep warm in the oven.
10. Reduce the cooking liquid by three-quarters; add the saffron. After half a minute add the cream, and reduce the sauce by half again.
11. Arrange the fish on four serving plates and pour the sauce over it.
12. Place the julienne of vegetables in a wire sieve, and hold it in a big pot of boiling water for 10 to 15 seconds only. Take out, shake dry and sweat in a frying pan in about 15 g of butter . . . no more, or the vegetables will become greasy. Garnish the plates of fish with the cooked julienne of vegetables and tomato and serve at once.

HILTON-RICHFIELD

Sounds like a lot of work and a complicated method, but it isn't at all. Stephen Pidgeley is the executive sous chef of The Carlton and he has explained each step simply but thoroughly. Saffron is always best in its original threads. Terribly expensive, of course, but you only use a few threads at a time for each recipe if the quality of the saffron is good. Failing that, flakes and powder are available, but not as satisfactory.

Daybreak at Nederburg, in the Paarl Valley.

Imagine a wine that captures the delicate copper-pink blush in a dawn sky and the crisp freshness of the new day.

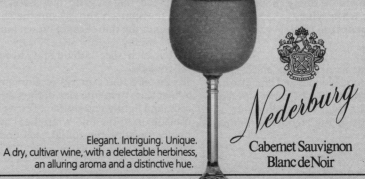

Elegant. Intriguing. Unique.
A dry, cultivar wine, with a delectable herbiness,
an alluring aroma and a distinctive hue.

From the Winemasters.

Nederburg

Cabernet Sauvignon
Blanc de Noir

We'd like to share Nederburg with you.
Call us at (02211) 623104 to arrange your visit.

Roulade of Smoked Salmon and Kingklip
(by Chef Glynn Sinclair)

INGREDIENTS:
4 nice slices of smoked salmon, about
    25 cm x 15 cm
200 g kingklip, filleted
4 large spinch leaves, stems removed
250 ml fresh cream
pinch of grated nutmeg
30 g butter
3 egg whites
50 g sliced chanterelles, canned or
    bottled (or ordinary brown
    mushrooms, if necessary)
salt and pepper to taste
THE SPINACH SAUCE:
50 g spinach
250 ml fresh cream
grated nutmeg
1 medium onion, finely chopped
60 ml dry white wine
salt and pepper to taste

METHOD:
1. Cut the kingklip into small strips, place in a food blender and liquidise for a few seconds, until it becomes a purée.
2. Add the egg white slowly to the. kingklip while the blender is in operation.
3. Add the fresh cream and blend.
4. Remove kingklip mousse from the blender and season to taste with salt and pepper. Stir in the grated nutmeg, and reserve.
5. Boil a large pan of water. When boiling fiercely, drop in the spinach leaves with most of the stem removed. Push into the water with a wooden spoon. Keep the lid off. Boil for no more than 10 seconds. Remove the spinach, and refresh it in a bowl of iced water.
6. Remove spinach leaves from the water and pat dry with a towel, or dry in a salad-spinner.
7. Lay out the salmon slices individually. Line each with spinach leaves.
8. Spread the kingklip mousse evenly over the spinach and lay out the chanterelles or the thin slices of brown mushrooms evenly.
9. Roll each slice individually, to form the roulade.
10. Prepare four squares of aluminium foil, at least twice the size of the salmon rolls, and lightly butter them. Place each roulade on to the foil, wrap them quite tightly, twisting the foil at each end to form a nice cylindrical shape, that should be completely airtight. Poach or steam for about 15 minutes.

THE SPINACH SAUCE:
1. Sweat the chopped onions in about 15 g of butter.
2. Add the white wine and reduce to about one-third of volume.
3. Add the fresh cream and once again reduce by half.
4. Blanch the spinach leaves in boiling salted water, as before. Squeeze out excess water and liquidise to a fine purée.
5. Add the spinach purée to the sauce, reduce to the desired consistency, and season to taste.

Town House Hotel ★★★ TYYY
60 Corporation Street,
Cape Town 8001
Telephone: (021) 45-7050
PO Box 5053, Cape Town 8000
Open daily
Fully licensed

Town House

*S*urprisingly pretty for a commercial hotel, cleverly furnished and decorated, and as comfortable a hostelry as you could ever expect to have three stars, The Town House proceeds on its placid path unmindful of the moaning that is heard from some of its four- and five-star colleagues about lower occupancy, higher costs, diminishing profits.

Francois Petousis, who owns the delectable Vineyard Hotel as well, knows what he is about. He is a dedicated hotelier who believes a friendly atmosphere coupled with personal service make a hotel, and these qualities bring the patrons back again time after time. Obviously, he's right. The regular patrons of The Town House are almost like members of a club.

It isn't only the atmosphere that Mr Petousis keeps warm and friendly: he provides all his amenities at remarkably low prices: what could be friendlier than that? Visitors to Cape Town often exclaim, in fact, in surprise at the reasonableness and value for money at the restaurant in this most pleasant of town hotels.

This is not the place to look for cult food, trendy dishes, fancy preparation and presentation. This is the place to expect, and to receive, good food, seriously cooked, and appetisingly served. The fish, particularly, receives meticulous attention from the kitchen. It is never over-cooked (sadly, a feature of so many restaurants) and always carefully seasoned.

This is a very popular restaurant. It isn't hard to see why.

Salmon and Avocado Cornettes with Sprouts

INGREDIENTS:
4 medium slices smoked salmon
1 ripe avocado
30 ml cream
45 ml mixed sprouts, toasted lightly in
   a pan, turning all the time
Fingers of crisp, buttered wholemeal
   toast
8 large lettuce leaves
15 ml lemon juice
a little cream cheese
Salt and freshly ground black pepper
   to taste

METHOD:
1. Twist the salmon into triangle-shaped cornettes. Arrange on individual plates on the lettuce leaves.
2. Make a purée of the avocado, lemon juice, cream and cream cheese (which always adds an interesting consistency).
3. Lift up one corner of the salmon cornette. Pipe avocado cream into the corner and sprinkle with extra salt and pepper, and the toasted sprouts.
4. Serve with fingers of crisp buttered wholewheat toast.

HILTON-RICHFIELD
A pleasant dish for a starter or a party snack. Two ideas for ringing the changes.
1. Instead of smoked salmon, use slices of the marvellous smoked marlin coming in from Mauritius. It's expensive, but delicious.
2. Instead of using cream cheese, use a soft, fresh Greek Feta cheese, well-creamed with the cream and lemon-juice, and garnish with tiny black olives. Give it a good Greek name, such as "Paratathemos". It doesn't mean a thing; it's simply a made-up, Greek-sounding name, but some easily impressionable people might be impressed.

Cape Salmon with Spring Herb Butter

INGREDIENTS:
4 fillets of very fresh, large Cape
  salmon
2 carrots very finely chopped
lemon juice to taste
finely chopped chives
8 young carrots cut raw in the shape of
  thin lozenges
500 mℓ beaten butter (see "Standard
  Recipes")
15 mℓ chopped dill
watercress
salt and freshly ground white pepper

METHOD:
1. Using a sharp knife, cut the fish fillets into large chunks, fairly short and thick.
2. Put the fish chunks side by side, close together, on a large baking sheet.
3. Heat the oven to 250°C.
4. In a pan of simmering salted water, cook the lozenge-shaped carrots.
5. Prepare the beaten butter, adding lemon juice to taste. Correct seasoning and add the fresh chopped herbs. Keep warm.
6. At the last possible moment before required at the table, slightly moisten the fish on the baking tray by sprinkling with a little water. Put the tray in the middle of the very hot oven and cook for about 8 to 10 minutes.
7. Remove the fish and, with a large metal spatula, arrange on heated, very large . . . preferably hollowed . . . individual plates. Cover at once with the herb butter. Sprinkle the dish with the finely diced carrots and the watercress, and serve.

> **HILTON-RICHFIELD**
> *Again, here's a recipe whose simplicity disguises its subtlety. Fresh dill isn't always there in the shops. Try instead some chopped fresh tarragon (Chinese parsley, dhunia) or sweet basil. The strong herbs go well with Cape salmon without swamping its flavour.*

R. Ward '86

29 Gillespie Street,
Durban 4001
Telephone: (031) 37-0264
Closed Mondays
Unlicensed

Villa d'Este

*E*nrico Ferrari is an aristocrat of the Italian kitchen in the same way that his famous namesake rules the roost of fast and sporty motor-cars. The Ferrari roadster is a "character" among cars: Enrico is a "character" among restaurateurs.

He is an outgoing, ebullient, extrovert man, who runs his little trattoria just the way he wants to. Until recently, the walls of his room, the beams across the ceiling, every available space, were filled with messages from delighted customers, in at least 20 major languages. We have not yet seen the Villa d'Este in its new suit of clothing, and we hope the atmosphere remains relaxed and informal, with its "anima romana" and its strong aromas of oil, garlic, rosemary and cooking shellfish.

It would be a sorry story if all that could be said about the Villa d'Este was the personality of its "padrone". There's more to it than that. The Villa d'Este is a rarity, in that it's an Italian restaurant that pays no attention whatsoever to South African tastes, and provides real "cucina italiana", flavoured and spiced with the full pungencies of that marvellous cuisine. Get Enrico to bake you a whole, fresh linefish, with olive oil and white wine, garlic and rosemary, in his pizza oven. And we challenge you to tell us where you can find Italian cooking better than that.

At the entrance is a refrigerated counter with wonderful goodies on display. Big crayfish, huge prawns, giant langoustines. Yes, Signor Ferrari will be glad to cook them for you, but ask the price first. They are liable to be expensive. Not quite as costly, but just as delicious, are his cold salad of calamari, his stuffed fresh mussels waiting to be shoved under the grill, and other typically Italian concoctions.

The place is not licensed. So take along with you the best bottle of imported Italian vino you can find – the cooking deserves it.

Baked Fish "Ferrari"

INGREDIENTS:
whole rock cod or red roman,
  1,5 to 2 kg
300 mℓ dry white wine
parsley, chopped, for garnish
60 mℓ olive oil
30 mℓ lemon juice
THE STUFFING:
45 mℓ fresh, softened butter
2 to 4 cloves garlic, pounded or
  pressed
5 mℓ rosemary, chopped
salt and pepper to taste

METHOD:
1. Have the fishmonger scale and clean the fish thoroughly, leaving head, tail and skin on.
2. Blend the butter with well-chopped fresh rosemary, garlic, salt and pepper.
3. With a short and very sharp knife, cut along the fish's backbone and make a deep slit. Press the butter, garlic and rosemary stuffing into it. Leave a little stuffing over and rub it into the surface of the entire fish.
4. Place the fish in a baking pan. Pour the olive oil over it. (You can use ordinary oil, but it won't taste as good.) Bake in oven preheated to 180°C for approximately 20 minutes.
5. Remove pan from the oven, and quickly pour over the fish the white wine and the lemon juice. Return to the oven and allow to cook for a further 10 minutes.
6. Heat a large serving platter and place the fish on it. Sprinkle with chopped parsley. Bring to the table as hot as possible and serve by cutting portions from the whole fish . . . two from one side, then turn over and cut two from the bottom side.

HILTON-RICHFIELD
Ideal with this fish would be a small baking dish full of thinly sliced potatoes, pre-soaked in an oil-and-butter mixture, flavoured with salt, pepper and rosemary leaves, baked in the oven at the same time. When serving, you may find it awkward carving portions while the fish is in the middle of the table, where it belongs. True, after a couple of stabs it does look as if the gannets have got at it, but not even an expert fish-carver can keep it neat and tidy. Don't worry! The aroma and taste will overcome any aesthetic reservations!

Seaman's Soup alla Livornese

(In the Leghorn style)

INGREDIENTS:
2 fish heads: rock cod, steenbras, or
  similar
1 leek (white only) finely chopped
3 ripe, peeled tomatoes, chopped
1 to 4 chillies, depending on size and,
  strength
1 stick celery, finely chopped
1 large carrot, finely chopped
2 cloves garlic, pounded or pressed (or
  6 whole cloves, used just as they are)
a few dashes olive oil
salt and pepper to taste

METHOD:
1. Place the fish heads in a deep pot and
just cover with water. Boil. Remove scum
2 or 3 times if necessary. If water level
falls to below the fish, add more water
. . . slowly, so as not to stop the boiling
process.
2. Remove from water and drain, but do
not allow to get too cool. With a small-
bladed knife, remove all the flesh from
the heads, and reserve.
3. Place the chopped celery, leek, carrot
and tomato in a saucepan. No water
needed: the tomato provides enough liquid. Add garlic, salt and pepper, and
chillies (see note below). Add the stock in
which you boiled the fish heads, and the
flaked fish (having discarded all the
bones), and cook together for about 20 to
30 minutes.
4. Serve in soup plates, and at the table
add a dash or two of pure olive oil into
each plate. "Buon appetito!"

HILTON-RICHFIELD
*Make sure you know the strength of
the chillies you use. Their fierceness
varies from type to type. Finger-
length red chillies usually have a
smoother taste than green ones.
Triangular or heart-shaped chillies
are fiercely hot. The tiny "Devil
Chillies" are best consigned to Hades,
where they belong!*

*Fish heads aren't everyone's cup of
joy. It's the gelatine in them that
makes such a wonderful soup. In any
case, your guests don't see the darn
things: only you. Put your prejudices
behind you and pick the flesh out of
the heads with determined glee.*

R·W.

235

Vineyard Hotel ★★★ TYYY
Protea Road, Newlands 7700
Cape Town
Telephone: (021) 64-2107
PO Box 151, Newlands 7725
Open daily
Fully licensed

The Vineyard

*U*ndoubtedly one of the most beautiful hotels in the country, even taking into account its three stars. Those stars are awarded for the number and type of the amenities offered; not for quality of performance. If quality were the criterion, its stars might become a veritable galaxy!

It's a very old building and is actually a National Monument. The rooms are comfortable, though, and all the equipment and accoutrements are thoroughly modern. The view of the Mountain from the back rooms, over the garden sweeping down to the river, is delightful, even when it's raining (and when isn't it raining here in Newlands?).

The owner of this delightful hostelry – and of the equally delightful Town House in central Cape Town – is Francois Petousis, one of the most popular hoteliers in South Africa. His warm smile and friendly greeting are genuine – they are not put on to conceal a cold commercial heart. Mr Petoussis is that rare figure, a truly warm and friendly man.

Because he enjoys people, and loves to host them, he has deliberately kept down the costs and prices of his food. The restaurant is elegance itself, and the dishes are expertly cooked and served, but at prices that are considerably lower than they might be.

When the rooms are fully occupied, the restaurants and bar swinging along with activity, the staff extended to the limits of hospitality, we wonder if the ghost of Lady Anne Barnard might not be lurking there somewhere amid the antiques and the paintings. After all, it was her house once. We think possibly she might approve, if what history tells us of that good lady's social proclivities is true!

Grilled Linefish with Fresh Ginger and Mango Curry Mayonnaise

INGREDIENTS:
4 portions linefish, filleted
SEASONING:
15 mℓ salt
2 cloves garlic, crushed very fine
15 mℓ fresh fennel or dill, finely
  chopped
5 mℓ grated lemon rind
30 mℓ freshly ground black pepper
10 mℓ ginger root, finely chopped
30 mℓ lemon juice
60 mℓ olive oil
THE SAUCE:
75 mℓ cream
5 mℓ mild curry powder
15 mℓ mango chutney
75 mℓ mayonnaise
15 mℓ shredded coconut
15 mℓ chives, chopped
THE GARNISH:
rice cooked your own way
mixed green salad with herb
  vinaigrette
red and green bell peppers, sliced

METHOD:
1. Mix the seasoning ingredients well together. Some time before grilling the fish, rub the seasoning mixture well into the fish portions.
2. Put the sauce ingredients into a blender and blend until creamy.
3. Grill the fish and serve with the red peppers, your rice dish, the mango curry mayonnaise on the side, and a mixed salad with herb vinaigrette dressing.

HILTON-RICHFIELD
Though the Vineyard Hotel is a National Monument, there's nothing antidiluvian about their cuisine! This is a lovely, light dish, in keeping with the principles of nouvelle cuisine, cuisine moderne, cuisine reformée and all the other names that have been given over the years to the lighter style of French cookery. This recipe, nevertheless, has a fine feel of Cape cookery; what with the curry and the chutney and the spices.

Graça was the vino.

There are many ways of enjoying Graça.
But here's a simple recipe that seems to work every time.
First, take a tableful of friendino's of assorted sexes, as shown. Place in a warm, cheerful and not too sedate ambience.
Mix in the speciality of the house. In this case, freshly caught line fish.
And throughout, marinade generously with the most important ingredient of all.
Graça.
A crisp, earthy white wine.
With a very slight sparkle. A decidedly different taste. And an unusual effect on what happens around it.

Graça. The talking, eating, drinking, laughing, singing, sharing wine.

Produced in the Republic of South Africa.

Vineyard Seafood Salad with Warm Orange Sauce

a selection of linefish (cubed), crayfish tails, shrimps (cleaned and deveined), prawns (cleaned and deveined), mussels, tuna and calamari

THE SAUCE:
juice of 1 orange
½ spring onion, finely chopped
5 mℓ chopped mint
80 mℓ thick cream
1 egg yolk (perhaps)
1 small cube cold butter (for sauce)
15 mℓ lemon juice
1 small bay leaf
80 mℓ good vegetable stock (see "Standard Recipes")
5 mℓ malt vinegar
15 mℓ butter
few drops of sesame oil (optional)

THE GARNISH:
thin julienne of cucumber, white button mushrooms (raw), carrot and celery
1 large, whole English cucumber, sliced very thinly (preferably in the food processor)

METHOD:
1. Make your selection of fish, shellfish and calamari. Cut it into bite sizes. Keep in a bowl, dripping a few drops of Chinese sesame oil over it. Toss until all pieces are coated. Keep aside until about half-an-hour before serving.

2. Make your julienne of cucumber, mushrooms, carrots and celery. All strips should be of equal dimensions.

3. Score down the entire length of the cucumber, leaving skin on, making six or seven grooves, each about 1 or 2 mm thick. This will give the slices a serrated edge and add to the appearance of the dish. Slice the cucumber thinly and evenly in the processor. Arrange the slices right round the edge of a serving dish, as regularly as possible. Mix the julienned items together and spread on the base of the dish, inside the ring of cucumber.

4. To make the sauce, put the orange juice, lemon juice, chopped spring onion, bay leaf, chopped mint and vegetable stock in a saucepan. Reduce over a rapid heat until the volume has diminished by two-thirds.

5. Add 80 mℓ thick cream and simmer again for 5 minutes. Add the malt vinegar. If the sauce is not of good pouring consistency because it is too thin, whisk in the yolk of an egg. Be careful not to bring to the boil again, or the egg will separate. Now stir or whisk in the cold butter to enrich the sauce, again taking care not to let it boil. Keep warm.

6. Now that everything else is ready, prepare to cook the fish. Steam or poach it, but take care to remove from the heat while still undercooked. The cooking process will continue as it cools. This way all the flavour is not cooked away into the poaching liquid. Try to cook the fish at the last moment before serving: certainly not more than 15 to 20 minutes.

HILTON-RICHFIELD

We are glad that the chef at The Vineyard has warned about overcooking the fish. South African home cooks tend to overcook everything. A steak that is overcooked still retains some flavour and quality: we even understand that there are one or two odd people around who have actually developed a taste for overcooked meat. But with fish, don't do it! Rather undercook. When you're nearly ready to serve, if you can see that the fish has not cooked enough while being kept warm, simply pop it back in the warming drawer for five minutes or so. The retained heat will warm it through and bring it to the cooked consistency you need.

Mariner's Wharf,
The Harbour, Hout Bay 7872
Telephone: (021) 790-1100
Open daily
Wine & Malt Licence

Wharfside Grill

A vision, a dream, a brave notion in one man's head, triumphantly realised and already, after a short time, receiving accolades of praise from all quarters. That's Mariner's Wharf, arising from old buildings on the Hout Bay harbourside, with its fresh fish market, its emporium of fish-connected groceries, souvenirs, hats and clothing, its two (soon to be three) restaurants.

Stanley Dorman, the fifth generation of a family of Hout Bay trawlermen and shipowners, must burst with pride as he sees his dream-come-true so heavily patronised, the crowds queueing at the fish take-away, the lines patiently waiting to be allowed into the Wharfside Grill. The concept is so large, the realisation so unexpected, that one imagines even the seagulls swarming over the boats in the harbour are wondering what has hit staid, quiet, artistic old Hout Bay!

You can go straight into the restaurant and order from the menu, or you may stride purposefully into the shop, choose your fresh fish from the ice on the counter, or your live lobster, oysters, mussels or what-have-you from the sea-water tanks, and have it sent in to be cooked for you as you wish.

The rough-and-ready ambience, reminiscent of the old days at sea, is the result of clever design and planning, but it tends – successfully – to sink the differences between people. All are treated equally here at the wooden tables; Cabinet ministers, ambassadors, the glitterati of the north and the south, and ordinary folk out for the day, while in the evenings the minstrel strums and sings his nautical ditties to the delight of all.

We confidently predict that Mariner's Wharf will soon become a tourist mecca, as inviting an amenity as Gold Reef City has become in Johannesburg. With the addition, of course, of the sea, the ships and the wonderful relics of seafaring days that clamour for attention from every wall.

In San Francisco there's Fisherman's Wharf. And now in Cape Town there's Mariner's Wharf.

Paella Pescatore

INGREDIENTS: (For 6)
375 g rice
2 crayfish tails
1 kg kingklip, cubed to about 3 cm size
450 g shrimps
300 g mussels
1 green pepper, sliced
150 g button mushrooms (optional)
375 ml water
pinch saffron threads
5 g fresh thyme
1 ℓ court-bouillon (see "Standard Recipes")
200 mℓ olive oil
2 medium onions, sliced
150 g cleaned calamari, sliced into rings
250 mℓ dry white wine
5 g ground turmeric
3 cloves garlic, crushed
freshly ground black pepper
salt to taste

METHOD:
1. Put the rice on to cook your own favourite way.
2. Separate the tails from the crayfish. (Reserve the bodies for other purposes, such as making bisque, crayfish sauce, etc.)

3. Poach the tails in a court-bouillon. Allow to cool in the liquid. Remove the tails and cube into bite sizes. (Freeze the court-bouillon for use again later.)
4. Clean and devein the shrimps, and poach in some of the court-bouillon. Allow to cool. Remove. (Reserve the liquid, as above.)
5. In a deep pot, steam the mussels until they open. Discard any that do not open.
6. Heat 50 mℓ of the olive oil. Brown the cubes of kingklip. Do not overcook. Remove while still firm, drain, and put to one side.
7. Add the rest of the oil, heat, and sauté the onions, sliced pepper and the crushed garlic. Add rice, saffron, turmeric and thyme. Add the water and wine, only a very little at a time. Simmer for ten minutes.
8. By now the rice should be nearly cooked. Place the browned kingklip pieces in the rice, together with all the other ingredients. Toss to mix well. Heat through for ten minutes. Add salt and pepper to taste.
9. Serve with a French salad and some garlic bread.

HILTON-RICHFIELD

This recipe is quite far distant from a traditional paella of Spain, in which seafood, chicken, chorizo sausage and rice are cooked together. Personally, we would add plenty of garlic, but of course that's not to everyone's taste. Is it the aftermath of garlic that's offensive to you? Don't you enjoy having that marvellous tang on your breath — or are you sensitive to other people's expressions as you breathe their way? Moenie panic nie! Suck a couple of Amplex tablets, those tiny green chlorophyll pills from England. Or (more enjoyable) eat a couple of pieces of the strongest cheese you can find, such as very mature cheddar. Or even several sprigs of fresh parsley. Sweetness and light will follow!

Mariner's Chowder

INGREDIENTS:
6 crayfish bodies (shells, legs, but no tails)
Backbone and head of a fish (kob, yellowtail or kingklip preferred)
1 bunch cooking celery
4 bay leaves
150 mℓ medium dry sherry
3 medium onions
50 g cake flour
2 ℓ water
100 g fresh parsley
12 whole black peppercorns
250 mℓ cream
30 g butter
salt and pepper to taste

METHOD:
1. Place the crayfish bodies, fish head, fish backbone, celery, parsley, bay leaves, peppercorns and onions in a pot. Cover with water. Bring to the boil and simmer for 3 hours. Remove scum. Strain through muslin or a cloth, allowing liquid to drip. Put this stock to one side.
2. Make a roux by melting the butter in a pan and blending in the cake flour. Do not allow the butter to colour.
3. Add the prepared fish stock and cream alternately, a little at a time, stirring so that no lumps form. Simmer for 2 minutes. Add the sherry. Season with salt and pepper to taste.

HILTON-RICHFIELD
Served piping hot, this is satisfyingly robust fare. The finishing touch, we believe, would be a whole heap of croûtons flavoured with plenty of garlic. Wonderful for a one-course supper dish. This will serve at least 6 to 8.

R·W.

245

R. Ward '86

Bridge Road,
Milnerton, Cape Town 7441
Telephone: (021) 52-2423
PO Box 202, Milnerton 7435
Closed Sundays and Monday evenings
Fully licensed

Wooden Bridge

Cornishman Arthur Williamson runs this highly successful establishment, now that owner Pieter Maas has sadly passed on. Arthur was the chef here for some years, and it is always pleasant to see a good chef come out of the kitchen into the realms of management. It means, among other things, that the standard of the kitchen is always under an eagle eye.

What a wonderful situation for a restaurant! Virtually under the Milnerton lighthouse, with a wide view over the waters of Table Bay to the city and the mountain beyond, "spectacular" is a mild term for the view.

As is to be expected, fish and seafood are prominent on the menu. In fact, says Mr Williamson, fresh fish accounts for 65 percent of the food sold here. And that doesn't include the items on the menu-list, but only the "specials" that depend on what comes in from the trawlers of Mossel Bay and the fishermen along the coast.

The prices both of the food and the wines are surprisingly low. After a couple of preliminary toasts at the pleasant bar, a low bill at the tables keeps the accounting for the evening within sensible bounds! This is a favourite rendezvous for businessmen at lunchtime and the surroundings are so romantic that, in the evenings, intimate têtes-à-tête at the tables are a frequent sight.

The Wooden Bridge (the original structure is not so heavily used now that the concrete ribbons of the city have extended to the front door of the restaurant) has established itself as one of the most popular middle-of-the-road dining-rooms of the Cape. Pieter Maas would have been proud to see how well his family and his colleagues are carrying on the tradition he founded.

Sole "Wooden Bridge"

INGREDIENTS:
4 x 300 g soles, skinned, whole, side
  bones off
150 g Norwegian frozen shrimps
30 mℓ chopped parsley
250 g lemon butter compound
50 mℓ oil
50 g capers
3 lemons, peeled and segmented
250 g seasoned flour
100 g butter
SEASONED FLOUR:
mix flour with 5 mℓ each salt, pepper,
  paprika
LEMON BUTTER COMPOUND:
Beat 250 g softened butter in blender
until fluffy. Add juice of 2 lemons and
beat until juice is absorbed into butter.
Add 2 whole eggs. Beat at high speed
for further 2 minutes.

METHOD:
1. Spread the seasoned flour on a large
plate. Place the soles in it, patting the fish
so that flour is firm on the surface. Shake
off excess flour.
2. Heat the combined oil and butter in a
pan and fry the fish until golden-brown
on each side.

3. Remove to serving plates. Arrange lemon segments on each fish.
4. Divide capers and shrimps into equal portions and arrange on top of the fish, together with the lemon segments. Top with helping of lemon butter compound and grill until the butter turns golden brown. Sprinkle with chopped parsley.

> ### HILTON-RICHFIELD
> *This simple recipe becomes eloquent by using really good shrimps. We know of none better than the Norwegian frozen shrimps (there are occasionally some from Iceland and Greenland, too) sold by Woolworths. Unlike most frozen fish, they retain a strong flavour which comes through even after cooking. And lemon butter compound seems to have a much nicer effect than if you simply used melted butter with lemon juice in it.*

Calamari Casserole

INGREDIENTS:
1,2 kg calamari, cut into rings
2 onions, chopped finely
2 sticks celery, diced finely
1 bay leaf
15 mℓ chopped parsley
500 mℓ fish velouté (see "Standard
   Recipes")
150 mℓ riesling wine
salt and pepper to taste
2 tomatoes, blanched, skinned,
   deseeded and chopped
3 cloves garlic, chopped and crushed
1 leek, sliced thinly
18 black olives, depipped
5 mℓ chopped thyme
75 g butter
150 ml cream

METHOD:
1. Melt the butter in a pan and sauté the garlic, onion, celery and leek.
2. Add the riesling, bring to boil, and reduce by three-quarters.
3. Add cream. Reduce until the cream begins to thicken.
4. Add the calamari. Bring back to the boil, then add the tomatoes, olives, bay leaf, thyme and the fish velouté.

5. Check seasoning. Add chopped parsley. Serve immediately with rice.
Total cooking time: 5 minutes.

HILTON-RICHFIELD
Calamari has certainly become South Africa's favourite "continental" seafood. We wonder if this would have been the case if it were always called "squid" (which we once saw spelled on the menu-card in a Portuguese restaurant as "skweed"). This is a real Mediterranean dish, needing a robust white wine to complement it. And do, please, remember that overcooking calamari makes them feel like miniature General Tyres.

249

R. Ward '86

Zoo Lake Gardens,
Parkview, Johannesburg 2193
Telephone: (011) 646-8807
Closed Sunday evening and Mondays
Fully licensed

Zoo Lake

This splendid restaurant must surely qualify for consideration as the most beautiful in South Africa. With its contrasting rooms, its huge windows looming over the water of Zoo Lake while birds strut over the lawns, with its "gemütlich" air of middle-European comfort and elegance, this is a restaurant on the grand scale, in the finest traditions of European hospitality.

And everything runs with the precision of a Swiss watch. Presiding over it all with a genial air, the epitome of a classical "mine host", is Hermann Muetschler, who has run the Zoo Lake for 17 years.

His brigade of waiters, from the elegantly-suited young gentlemen from Europe down to the last commis, are arguably the best-performing group in the business. This is a serious room, they indicate, where what you are going to eat and the way it is going to be served are matters of great moment.

The food will not let your expectations down. Rudi Kegel, the excellent chef, has been here for 14 years now, and his techniques are solid, his touch light, and his versatility enormous. French cuisine is the mainstay of the menu, but Mr Muetschler will occasionally give the nod to a dish or two from his own part of the world – cooked, of course, to the high and exacting standards of the kitchen.

The wine-list is superb. Everything you would expect is here, including probably the best cellar of German wines to be found in South Africa, nestling alongside the finest marques of France and the Cape. Cognacs, liqueurs, cigars are here in profusion: in fact, everything to flatter the sybaritic tastes of the Zoo Lake's upper-crust patrons can be found right at your elbow.

A very superior restaurant, this, that goes on from year to year, unchanged, unflustered, the very epitome of European excellence.

251

Prawns à la Brochette "Fergie"

INGREDIENTS:
8 – 20 prawns, depending on size,
   cleaned, shelled and deveined
16 – 20 small rashers of bacon
16 – 20 prunes, pitted
5 mℓ curry powder
extra pineapple julienne, for garnish
250 g butter
250 mℓ long grain rice
125 mℓ pineapple, diced
parsley, chopped
salt and pepper to taste

METHOD:
1. Wrap each prawn, lightly seasoned
with salt and pepper, in a rasher of bacon.
2. On skewers, place alternately a prune
and a prawn. Push together firmly but
not tightly. Sauté lightly in 100 g of the
butter until golden-brown.

RICE:
3. Cook the rice according to your favourite method. Just before it is ready,
add a pinch of mild curry powder. Stir in
well. Add diced pineapple and the left-
over prunes.
4. Remove the rice from the cooking-pot

and sauté it together with the fruit in
100 g of the remaining butter.

SERVING:
5. On an oval or oblong platter, place a
bed of the rice in the centre, to extend just
beyond the length of the skewered
prawns. On each heap of rice, place a
skewer of prawns and prunes.
6. Sauté the pineapple julienne in remaining butter, then sprinkle along the
top surface of the skewered prawns. Finish with some finely chopped parsley.

HILTON-RICHFIELD
*Chef Rudi Kegel, who has been at the
Zoo Lake's ovens for 17 years now,
created this delightful dish specially
for our book, at the time of the Royal
Wedding.*

  *Do you have difficulty in getting
the food off the skewer when it has
been well-cooked? The technique is
simple. Instead of trying to pull the
bits of food off with a fork, lay the
skewer flat on the plate, ring-end
outwards. Hold down firmly with a
fork, and then pull the skewer away
from the food — not the food away
from the skewer.*

Kingklip à la Blanquette

INGREDIENTS:
4 pieces of filleted kingklip, about
    200 g each
250 mℓ cream
2 bananas, ripe
30 mℓ Dijon-type mustard
plain rice, cooked your own way
100 mℓ fish velouté (see "Standard
    Recipes")
½ onion, chopped
250 mℓ white wine
250 mℓ whipped cream
salt and pepper to taste

METHOD:
1. In a large pan, pour in the white wine, lightly seasoned. Add fish. Cook lightly. When done, remove the fish and keep it warm.
2. Reduce the wine by two-thirds. Add the cream. Add the fish velouté. Reduce by one-third.
3. Add French mustard, stirring all the time. Check seasoning.
4. Finally add the whipped cream, and stir. This will give you a smooth, rich "mousseline".
5. Place the kingklip, which has been kept warm, on a serving dish. Slice the ripe bananas thinly and place on top of the fish. Cover the fish and banana with the sauce. Glaze under the grill.
6. Pack the cooked rice in an oiled or buttered timbale. Empty out one portion on to each plate before serving the fish.

HILTON-RICHFIELD
Every kitchen should have a few of the tiny, shaped containers called "timbales" (although the word covers a variety of different-sized containers, too). Before use, spread a tiny amount of softened butter or oil inside each one. This will help the rice, or whatever you have packed into the timbale, to come out easily. It's one of those little touches of presentation that make your cooking seem very expert. There are little cone-shaped moulds, too, that are known as "darioles".

Index to Recipes